what
you've got
is
what
you want

adam e. jukes

FREE ASSOCIATION BOOKS

First published in 2016 by
Free Publishing Limited

Copyright © 2016 Free Publishing Limited

A CIP Catalogue of this book is available from
the British Library

ISBN: 978-1-8534321-8-7

Cover design by
Matt Maguire at Candescent Press
Initial concept by Kaleb Rose

Typeset by
www.chandlerbookdesign.co.uk

Printed in Great Britain by
4 Edge Limited

DEDICATED TO
Pamela Rose

CONTENTS

Foreword

As usual when a book is complete, I need to thank all the people without whom it would never have been completed, or would have been a very different book. Having said that, everything that follows is totally my responsibility. I have chosen to ignore or follow advice and that was my decision.

First, I need to thank all the patients and ex patients who gave permission to write accounts of their treatment. I have done my best to ensure that they cannot be identified, even by themselves and certainly not by their friends, family members and others. I hope I have done this, but my lawyers have been warned!

More personally, I want to thank Chris Scanlon, Morty Schatzman, Sally Barker, Tom Feldberg, and colleagues from my institute who took an interest in my scribbling and gave graciously of their time to comment on them. To the academic reader I also acknowledge the vast library of analytic writings on which I have drawn without reference. They range from Freud through Fairbairn [to whom I owe the idea of the feared object], Klein, Winnicott, Bowlby, Ballint, Kreeger, Waddell, Perls, Berne and others. The list is endless and I am prepared for the reproaches of all those if have forgotten to mention. However, I make a special thanks to my daughter Elli, from whom I learn so much that it is easy to forget.

Finally, huge gratitude is due to my son, Tom Jukes, who first suggested that an article I wrote deserved a slightly longer essay. Here it is. The original article is now the post-script to the book.

Introduction

There is no escape
There is simply the given and
There is nothing that we can do.
Harold Bloom

What's It All About?

Douglas Adams famously answered this in *The Hitchhiker's Guide to the Galaxy*, and the answer is 42! Unless you are a supermouse you'd probably think that's a crazy answer. What you are about to read here will probably seem just as crazy until you complete the whole book and eat the mooncheese.

The subtitle of the book could be, 'How to have the life you want' or 'Stop whingeing and enjoy the life you have!' This is not intended to be a self-help book, at least not in the way I understand that term. It isn't full of homework or positive thinking or standing in front of mirrors chanting or repeating mantras, with or without your clothes, one legged or otherwise. What it enjoins you to do, what I hope it will encourage you to do, is to think. I realise that thinking, particularly about the self, after a brief resurgence in the 1990's, is not so very popular these days. When I grew up it was all the rage. Higher education would be available to everyone, poverty would be eradicated. Science and its bedfellow, the white heat of technology, were the routes to this nirvana. They were going to lead us to the promised land where we'd never have to work again; no kids would starve or be beaten or neglected; war would be a historical curiosity and men and women would be indistinguishable from each other (already difficult in the 1960s and 70s if dress styles were anything to go by).

The problem was that this raised expectations to unrealistic levels. We could all have everything - providing we didn't look too closely at what it was that was supporting our consuming and our acquisitiveness. Oliver James calls it 'affluenza' and it could not have been better named. Right now we're all suffering from post viral fatigue syndrome as we individually and systemically pay the price for burning the candle at both ends.

For a while, all that consuming and acquisitiveness and greed stopped us thinking about what we were doing with our lives and our planet and our psyches. Now, however, it seems we have never been so interested in what goes on in our lives and in doing something to help ourselves. There was an explosion in psychological therapies over the last twenty years. Those were the therapies known as the 'talking cures' as opposed to others which involve medication or the laying on of hands or other parts of the body. Ironically though, reflection or thinking, as a route to change, is increasingly going out of fashion, largely under the influence of economic failure and austerity. Financial conditions have driven policy makers to look for short cuts and quick fixes. Currently, the most popular is Cognitive Behaviour Therapy, CBT for short, or therapy light as I think of it.

My thinking origins are somewhat complex, having started life as an academic social psychologist and with having trained in Gestalt therapy and Transactional Analysis. These are both schools of 'humanistic' therapy, a phrase which means they are concerned with the whole person, are non-judgemental and client-centred as opposed to illness-centred. It was only when I understood the intellectual and clinical limitations of humanistic approaches that I began to take an interest in the more intellectual psychotherapies, particularly psychoanalysis. It was not an easy journey for me and this book is as much an attempt to integrate what I learned all those years ago in my first [!] analysis as it is to disseminate those lessons with the overlay of thirty-five years of clinical practice. Above all I learned that I was not who I thought I was and that my behaviour was driven by feelings, thoughts, and impulses of which I had no conscious awareness. This was actually quite startling at first, as I am sure will be much of the contents of this book. We all think we know Freudian psychoanalysis. After all, hasn't Woody Allen made enough jokes about it? It is joked about because it is, simply, anxiety-provoking for anyone who has not experienced it and is afraid of it. Although this is not a book about psychoanalysis, it is informed by my own analytic training and years of practice. I wanted to make sense of what I had learned and eventually arrived at what I began to call 'The Mad Hypothesis' which was subsequently developed into a more complex model. Those developments are in what follows and I have tried to present them in a way which is accessible to people who are troubled by their lives and want to make changes but don't know where to begin. I hope this is a beginning for you.

1

The Mad Hypothesis

I have already mentioned The Mad Hypothesis in the introduction and here I intend to flesh it out a little. The Mad Hypothesis came to occupy a prominent place in all my groupwork and has subsequently informed a lot of my activity in individual work. Initially I used it only in men's groups but then it gained a foothold in my mixed gender groups as men transferred from one to the other and emigrated with the concept, so to speak. At first glance it does not seem very psychodynamic or analytic but I hope to show otherwise. I initially developed it in working with men who were involved in relationships which were full of 'malignant mirroring'. This is a situation in which two people reflect each other as monsters by repeatedly articulating how bad they each think the other is. The relationship is full of the accusative form – YOU! It is as if each holds up to the other a mirror in which the reflection projected is of someone who is irredeemably bad. The image one sees of oneself is of someone so bad that it is unrecognisable and indigestible. To identify with it would involve metabolising so much madness and/or badness that self-destruction would seem to be the only escape from the guilt.

What I learned from working with men and women in such relationships is that reality testing is impossible. Each member of the couple is struggling to locate and place the badness or madness in the relationship in the other. It is a very damaging and dangerous form of splitting (to be explained, but essentially it means separating the good from the bad such that they cannot be integrated) and leaves each person feeling very disturbed as they fail either to project the madness or to own it. The result is that the space between the couple is full of crazy projections which cannot be subjected to reality testing – even of the 'cut the baby in half' nature. The Mad Hypothesis became a way for a man to learn how to prevent the frequent and damaging quarrels, rows and violence that characterise such relationships.

At its simplest, the Mad Hypothesis is expressed as follows:

> **You are responsible for everything that is wrong with your relationship including any behaviour of your partner which you use to justify, excuse or in any other way account for your own behaviour towards him/her or the world in general.**

In my book, *Men Who Batter Women (1994)*, this was referred to as the Working Hypothesis. It has become the Mad Hypothesis because so many people said it was mad! Later, as I used it in my routine therapeutic work with men, both non-abusers and abusers, and with women, I changed it to include everything that was wrong with the person's life, not only their relationship, without any apparent loss of clarity, precision, utility or efficacy. I will describe how it is used in work with both abusive and non-abusive men and women. Although I am drawing a distinction here, I want to reiterate that I regard the differences between substantiated, abusing/controlling and non-abusing/controlling men to be quantitative, not qualitative, and that anything I say can be successfully applied to all.

Of course it is a mad idea. Simply on the face of it, it seems to portray the 'other' as no more than a cipher, a two dimensional cut-out in the person's world and as an object without desire or agency. Again, on the face of it we know this cannot be so even though we know from the speaking bitterness literature of the women's movement that many women actually experience themselves in just this way after years of abuse from the men they live with. We also know it from the narratives of friends and acquaintances with whom we empathise. However, as will become clear, it is not at all mad to hypothesise that anyone can view their partner as a two dimensional object suitable for use.

I actually tell most of my patients this hypothesis in the very first assessment session and I point out that it is mad because we all know that there are two people in a relationship. Actually, few abusive men know what a relationship is – they have no internal model of a couple and usually lack a theory of mind from which they can perceive their partner. Generally he will regard her as a servant, as someone who is there simply to fulfil his needs and meet his expectations. The sad reality is that the Mad Hypothesis is not so mad as it seems. It is really a sleight of hand, an acceptable, seeming lie I used in order to encourage people who see me to enter treatment. Actually it is not a new idea at all. Those of you who are familiar with Freud will recognise that the Mad Hypothesis is a condensation of his ideas concerning the primary and secondary gains from illness.[1]

I cannot over-emphasise the centrality or the importance to me of this hypothesis in my work with men's relationships with women and vice-versa. Without it, the work I do would be so different as to be unrecognisable. It has become a commonplace for men and women in treatment with me to mention the Mad Hypothesis. It is extremely rewarding to my narcissism when they say, as they do, that the Mad Hypothesis has actually 'saved their lives' in so many different ways. The method of use is transparently simple. It can also be applied by anyone in any difficult situation, not simply when violence or aggression is involved or threatened – in fact it is not an unreasonable premise on which to base any form of treatment for emotional distress, most especially with the 'worried well'. When the man or woman is in difficulty (in fact when any one of us is in difficulty) he or she will usually define himself as a victim of his partner or the situation. The person will invariably be experiencing a sense of injustice, for which of us does not, when we feel we are being victimised? In such circumstances we invariably become preoccupied with the motives and behaviour of our perceived persecutor.

I usually describe the Mad Hypothesis to patients as similar to the preparation of a storyboard for a film in which all the major events of the film are represented by a picture. From the very first picture, much, if not all, of the events that follow are given a set of meanings which are limited by that first picture. From his perspective, she has done something to him which he construes as persecuting, as in the coffee cup incident (see Chapter 6). Seen from the first picture, both his sense of injustice and his revenge are fully justified, understandable and legitimate, but his distress, his sense of injustice and his blaming of his partner has little or nothing to do with her behaviour. This cannot be over-emphasised with controlling men. Give an inch and they will take a mile! I know this will sound harsh to many, but abusive men, like all men, have used every explanation they can think of to explain their own and their partner's behaviour – but without success, or they would not be in my office. I introduce the Mad Hypothesis to the man (as I do with female patients) by simply asking him what is the missing picture before the one that he uses to begin his narrative. In other words, 'what did you do to make her/him do what s/he is doing to you in the first picture and which defines you as their victim?' It is at this point that the madness of the hypothesis becomes clear. In effect I am saying to him that he is not only responsible for his own behaviour but also for any behaviour of hers which he uses to justify any of his treatment of her. The mad hypothesis emerged out of the need for a rapid, radical intervention with violent men. Speed is essential; there are real people being hurt so long as the man continues to behave in his habitual ways, and this often includes children, whether or not they are the targets of the violence. Permanent damage results from simply being raised in such a family.

The Mad Hypothesis has been very successful with violent offenders to women and with female patients, whatever their difficulties. On the face of it this is quite hard to explain. Most of these men, indeed most people, have been to the very limit to avoid any suggestion that they are in any way responsible for their own behaviour. In fact every justification or excuse, every account they give is intended to achieve this one simple end: to deny responsibility. Why then should they take so readily to an idea which states explicitly that not only are they fully responsible for their own behaviour, but also for their victims'? Moreover, a victim who, until that moment, they had seen as their persecutor.

I think the first answer is that it confirms what people already know: that they are, in fact, responsible for pretty much everything that has gone wrong in the relationship and their lives. They know they are responsible for their violent and abusive behaviour, their failure in careers and friendships, but they are unable to acknowledge it either to themselves or to their partners. The main reason for this is, as Freud would have put it, the counter-transference. Their self-love or narcissism will not allow such a massive re-organisation of the self-image. Basically they would have to admit that they are, in some important senses, not a very nice person. This would involve too much guilt, shame, self-loathing and remorse. What the Mad Hypothesis allows is for people to acknowledge what they know to be the truth but in the presence of an 'expert' (who also happens to not be a woman!) who is simultaneously telling them that it is simply an experiment and not really the truth at all. I frequently attach it to a very simple description of systems theory and say something to the effect that it doesn't matter very much where we intervene in the system because a change in any of its components will change the whole system anyway. Naturally, not everybody takes to this readily. At this point some will say something to the effect that it isn't fair that he should take all the blame and that one of the reasons he behaves in the way he does is that she will never acknowledge she is in the wrong and he gets blamed for everything. Of course this is nonsense. The fact is that he is swollen with guilt about his behaviour and consequently believes himself to be persecuted by his victim. This is the only way he can account for his guilt ('she is blaming me all the time') and one of the few ways he can account for his behaviour. I'm usually content when men respond in this way because it leads us so effortlessly into their 'sense of injustice'.

Another reason why men/women are willing to work with the Mad Hypothesis is that it immediately offers a paradigm which gives them the experience of being in control (again!) and of being able to wield an influence on events which, up until that moment, they had felt were out of control. It should come as no surprise that I have found it to be a very helpful diagnostic tool insofar as it focuses me on the question of the primary and secondary gains from the symptom or 'illness'.

There is one important caveat: although I have no doubt that many women (and men) unconsciously seek out abusive partners or just people with whom they are unhappy, particularly when they have grown up in a home in which their father abused their mother or their parents abused each other, this in no way indicates that they have a conscious wish to be abused or maltreated or that they enjoy it when it happens, any more than rape fantasies indicate a wish to be raped. Nobody enjoys being hurt in any way however validating it may be for the unconscious Weltanschauung. I hasten to add, however, that masochism, of which more later, is not uncommon in victims.

My experience is that most people already use the Mad Hypothesis. There is one important difference in this use – in most people's version they are the victim of someone else who is responsible not only for their own behaviour but also 'mine'. In their accounts 'my behaviour' is a reaction to their provocation.

Let me illustrate with some examples.

Take the well known case of the 'pursuer wife and the distancer husband'. She has it that no matter how hard she tries to get close to him he always backs away; she feels frustrated and deprived. He has it that she never allows him to get close because she is always trying to force him to be close to her and he feels engulfed, swamped and devoured. Systemically this is rather simple. Each is causing the other's behaviour and each is blaming the other. He pathologises her need for intimacy, it's neurotic; and she pathologises his fear of intimacy, probably accurately. 'Who started it?' is a wholly irrelevant question. 'Do they want to change it?' is the issue. Actually in all my work [and that is mainly with non abusive men and women] it is usually whether *he* wants to change it. The solution is simple. He has to begin to approach her and do the analytic work required to confront his fear of intimacy or she has to begin to leave him alone, become more obscure and induce insecurity in him. This is a dreadful solution and not a long-term one.

Or take the case of the man who cannot have a conversation with his wife or listen to her because she is always repeating herself and getting angry with him. The question 'What do you do to make her repeat herself and get angry with you?' usually elicits the simple answer that he does not listen to her so that what he sees as an effect is actually a cause. This is usually referred to by men as the 'nagging' issue. Nagging is what women do to men after men have decided, unilaterally, that the conversation is over.

The informed reader will perhaps have begun to recognise the phenomenon familiar to communication theorists of 'the solution which is the problem'. This is the idea that when someone recognises a problem they usually attempt to solve it by doing more of what they have always done without recognising that this is the problem (those interested should take a look at *Change* by Watzlawick et al.).

Take the case of the man who complained that his wife did not want to have sex with him as often as he wanted. When asked if she ever requested sex, the reply was 'not for a very long time'. Again with a little probing it became evident that when she had made a request he had never responded positively. In effect his wife had never had any sex life except his. Is it any wonder she was less than co-operative? This is a good example of a man using a woman as a sexual object. It was evident he was afraid of sexual intimacy.

Let's look at a more complex example. This concerns a man who had not had a foreign holiday with his family for years because neither he nor his wife or children had up-to-date passports. He had reproached his wife constantly with her failure to renew them. He worked hard outside the home whilst she was a full-time wife and mother. He thought it not unreasonable that she should do what was required to see to the renewal. His reproaches had not always been quiet or non-intimidating. She suffered from a severe flight phobia and it was clear what her investment was in not having passports. His attitude to her phobia (she had more complex depressive problems also) was nothing short of contempt for her frailty and vulnerability (a mirror of his attitude to his own). She saw this as exactly the sort of support she had received from him on the odd occasions they had flown when they had passports. He had effectively abandoned her emotionally as soon as they booked a holiday whilst she went through days of panic and depression at the prospect of flying.

This lack of sensitivity and empathy, his emotional coldness, was typical of his treatment of her in their marriage. He had consistently rejected her attempts at intimacy to the point where she had built a life that did not involve him. Of course he complained bitterly about being excluded by her activities and blamed her for the lack of intimacy – he had never had to consider that this was his problem and that he had constructed a solution which enabled him simultaneously to avoid his fears and project the guilt and blame.

There is one patient, Dean, whom I remember well and his situation illustrates both the older and the newer forms of the Mad Hypothesis.

He is a highly intelligent and charming man with a generally good disposition. His profession requires high levels of diplomatic and mediating skills. In his fifties when he came to see me, he was married with pre-pubertal children.

He had married a talented woman whom he fell in love with even though he knew she was slightly depressed and unhappy. He believed he could see and bring out the non-depressed and happy person in her. He was going to rescue her. When he came to me it was because he was seriously thinking of leaving the marriage as it was making him so unhappy. He was deeply troubled by this impulse as he was close to his children and could not bear the thought of not being a full time father to them. His wife's depression was really getting him down. He had done everything he could think of to make her happy but she was more unhappy than the woman he had married. He described her as unaffectionate and non-tactile, except with the children with whom he thought also she was too harsh at times. Their sexual relationship had dwindled to almost nothing. It seemed the more he did to help, the more unhappy and withdrawn she became. It had reached the point where he had taken to reproaching her for being unhappy. They had attempted marital therapy but she had been too anxious to continue with it. The therapist, who knew of my work, referred the man to me because she thought he may be emotionally abusive. As he told his story I was thinking about the primary and secondary gains for him in this situation. It emerged that he had been sent to boarding school when he was about six years old and that he had been heartbroken at being separated from the mother he adored.

He simply could not understand why she had sent him away and he cried for months - which did not endear him to his schoolfellows. He made a couple of attempts to 'escape' the school but eventually settled down and repressed his grief. He did well at the school but remained deeply lonely. He remembers concluding, as a young teen, that he had to make his mother happy as his parents' marriage was volatile and unhappy. It eventually ended in divorce. He still adored his mother during his teens and eventually took real care of her financially when he became successful. However, he became increasingly tetchy and irritable with her as he became an adult. It emerged that he had been in love in his twenties and thirties but that those relationships had ended in odd circumstances even though he was still in love with the women and they with him.

What became clear, quite quickly, was that his current state of misery in the marriage was almost identical to what he had felt at school. He could not understand why the woman he had loved and for whom he had done so much could be so rejecting and so unhappy. He cried bitterly when the link was made, sobbing like the child he had been. He also recollected that he had kept his distance from his mother to protect himself from further rejection although he insisted that he always behaved happily around her.

As Dean continued to blame his wife for the state of his marriage I asked him if this was how it had been in the marital therapy. He agreed that he saw her as the problem and that if she could get fixed he believed everything would be okay. He laughed wryly when I asked if any of his attempts to fix her had been beneficial. At this point I suggested that maybe we could set up a thought experiment in which he was the cause of all the problems in the marriage and his wife's behaviour was a product of his treatment of her. I explained that this was a 'mad hypothesis' and he was quite taken with the idea and took to it with alacrity. Initially he wanted to think about why he would have done it; what were the pay-offs for him. I managed to get him to put this on hold - park it, as he said - and he started to think seriously what he might have done to make her so depressed and unhappy. In the weeks that followed he drew up a catalogue of behaviour that would account for her state of mind, but became increasingly bewildered as to why he would have done these things when all he had ever wanted, he thought, was to make her happy. However, he had begun to accept that his conscious intentions at the outset of the relationship may not have reflected what he wanted and that he did not know he wanted. So far so good!

Naturally his question about why he would want to produce the opposite of what he though he wanted needed to be addressed. It is a fairly simple question.

What do you get from living with an unhappy and depressed woman?

Addressing this required some courage. It meant Dean had to face the possibility that the outcomes he had were the outcomes he wanted. In fact this is true of anyone who enters long-term talking cures that place the unconscious at the centre of the endeavour. The 'pay-offs' are the apparently undesired outcomes he is living with: the loneliness, the sadness, the sexual frustration, the anger and resentment, the desire to escape, the sense of failure, etc. It is here that we get to the more complex version of the Mad Hypothesis although I will return to this basic version a little later.

These feelings were Dean's default settings. His behaviour was designed to take him back to all the painful feelings he had lived with as a child. I will come back to Dean in a little while after I have described the more complex version of the Mad Hypothesis that developed later in my work and in which 'default settings' play a central role.

I want to add simply that any doubts I might have held about the Mad Hypothesis were dispelled in a mixed gender analytic group when its validity was being discussed in critical terms. This was shortly after I had formulated the concept and was giving it its first public airing. The central attack concerned the majority feeling in the group that most of their behaviour was caused by their partners' treatment of them. I made a banal comment about how much they liked to occupy the victim position and have it validated by other members when it suddenly occurred to me that they were all, already, using the hypothesis except that in their version it was their partner who was responsible for his behaviour as well as her own. Not without some pleasure at my cleverness, I pointed this out and it provoked gales of laughter when I suggested that since they already believed the Mad Hypothesis was valid all I was suggesting was that they reverse it! I have repeated this observation many times in my individual work with men and women – with similar positive outcomes.

2

What you've got is
what you want

For many years I have worked clinically with men and women who "suffer" with disordered personalities. These are people who are difficult to categorise when compared with the largely "worried well" who populate the couches of therapists or analysts. In the main, they come because of difficulties with some aspect of their behaviour which is beginning to affect their lives and the lives of people close to them. Generally speaking, apart from the many problems involving perverse sexuality (which are many), they were pre-occupied with the problems they were having with their closest or most important relationships, both romantic and professional, including with their career - which I also regard as an "object" in the same sense in which I regard a person as an "object". In the course of working with them I developed the model of thinking and working which I found very useful and which brought palpable benefits for them - the Mad Hypothesis. At its simplest I would tell them that any problems they were having in relationships with any object were entirely a consequence of their behaviour and that any behaviour of the difficult object (career, boss, wife, husband, girlfriend, colleague, etc) was a product of the way they treated the object. Unsurprisingly this does not go down well. "But that's mad!" was a common response. Well, in a way, it is, from an intellectual point of view. "How," they would ask, "can I be responsible for other people's behaviour?"

My eventual answer was that since they regarded themselves as the victim of the "object's" behaviour and that their own behaviour was contingent on the way the object was treating them, they already believed the Mad Hypothesis and all I was suggesting was that they reverse the polarity. This is usually met with laughter as if they have been caught out with their hand in the biscuit tin! For many years I used this model with great effect as it encouraged my patients to take full responsibility for their behaviour and the apparently unintended consequence - the object's maltreatment of them.

I can see that the Mad Hypothesis is fraught with intellectual pitfalls but actually it is a very condensed model of many of Sigmund Freud's most compelling ideas and is really an encapsulation of the psychoanalytic process. It gets very murky for my patients when I eventually suggest to them that they may also be responsible for the internal world of the objects in their lives, when these objects are people rather than abstractions like "career" or "money". It does sound rather mad when they are asked to imagine that they want to create states of mind or thoughts and feelings in the minds of the people they relate to, and to cause them to behave in certain ways, and that they can actually achieve this with their behaviour. In fact I am telling them that they have to regard the "unintended" consequences as unconsciously intended. Here things get a little complicated. In order for this to make any sense I have to be able to demonstrate that there is an unconscious mind and that it has motives and intentions that are not accessible to conscious reflection. I will save this for the reader until later and simply ask that it is taken as read for the time being.

As I grew more comfortable with the concept and easy in its use it began to become more complex in my thinking and over the years I have refined it and expanded it so that it is now a three level model of human functioning and it is that model which is the theme of this work.

Its development began with my patients asking me different versions of a rather obvious question. "Are you telling me that I actually want these bad and painful things to happen to me?" Naturally the answer is that it is precisely what I am saying to them. At this point the questions come thick and fast (which is actually quite slow in psychotherapy real time) but they usually are reducible to a very simple one: "Are you saying that I want the pain?" I'm sure it is no surprise that many baulk at this point, and I have to say that it is a part of the process when extra care and patience is required. Coming to terms with this is not easy, but then growing up never is! The question is difficult to answer in a way that is easy to resonate with because it implies that there is enjoyment in suffering and the English language, particularly the psychoanalytic language (where "masochism" seems to provide a face valid explanation but actually avoids the question), lacks an easy vocabulary to render it simple. I have tried to substitute the word "enjoyment" with "pleasure" and "contentment" but have finally ended up with "satisfaction", a satisfaction derived from feelings of legitimacy or confirmation of beliefs about the way the world is, and a justification for being who one experiences oneself as being, in a very profound way - however painful or anxiety-provoking this may be.

There are additional benefits, none the least of which is masochism, which will become clear and these also provide powerful confirmation of some very deeply held beliefs which all human beings share. We are all expert psychologists. We have to be to survive the difficulties of growing up, however badly we achieve that doubtful status. The problem is that our expertise is flawed or skewed by early experiences and we have no insight into the biases these leave as a legacy in our adult functioning. Those flaws, their origins and consequences for our psychological expertise, will form a large part of what follows in this book.

At the risk of being repetitive, I will give more simple examples of The Mad Hypothesis before I disclose its development into the three level model I now use.

Example 1

A man who used to meet with his friends regularly to smoke dope continued to do so after he married and had children. He had promised his fiancée he would reduce the frequency of this after they were married. In the beginning he did so but after the birth of his children he felt very stressed and beleaguered and gradually increased its frequency until he was doing it three or four times a week - the same level as his pre-marital habit. His wife 'nagged and complained' at him about his going out and leaving her with the two small children until he got so fed up he would phone his friends and meet with them to smoke dope. It is not difficult to see how her behaviour is contingent on his, at least at the most transparent level. I should say that it would be just as useful to apply the model to her but gender differences, particularly in power, would probably render it far less effective in such circumstances.

Example 2

A middle aged woman who was constantly rejected by men and complained she could not find someone she loved. She met many men. She was beautiful and clever and men fell for her readily. She suffered from very low self-esteem and she quickly started rejecting the men she became attached to and engaged with passionately. She would complain about their lack of chivalry and bad manners from a very Victorian perspective. She would make excessive demands on their time and other resources and gradually reduce her sexual activity with them. The men would initially respond by escalating their attempts to regain her sexual favour and her initial passionate engagement by giving more and more until they finally would have had enough and leave her. The harder they tried, the more she rejected them. She had driven away every man in her life and some of them she missed desperately and regretted what she had done. She actually felt contempt for any man who was attracted to her as she felt so unlovable. This is a very transparent example of both a self-fulfilling prophecy and The Mad Hypothesis. It is also a good illustration of making the object feel and have a state of mind which was not their own. In this case she projected deep feelings of rejection and unworthiness in every one of her victims; feelings that belonged to her but which she was unable to feel, contain and metabolise. They were simply too painful for her.

Example 3

Similarly, a woman who had done rather well in her career but now felt thwarted by her boss, and the institution, in her ambitions. She complained about and to him rather often and he regarded her sufficiently highly to retain her and use her competencies. However, he was thwarting her ambitions and avoiding her as he could not tolerate her level of dissatisfaction with him and the institution they worked in. There is no doubt her perceptions of both were accurate but her response simply made her position more painful for her and the people around her and confirmed what she already believed about herself - that she was not wanted.

Example 4

A man who is neglectful or abusive to his partner and constantly bemoans her anger with him and believes that he is neglectful and abusive because she is rejecting and angry, when in fact her behaviour is an understandable response to his maltreatment of her. He seems to want to be loved for being hateful and he confirms what he already believes, that he is not lovable.

Example 5

The man or woman who suffers from profound and unresolved problems with dependency in relationships. These people are often referred to as co-dependent, not a concept I am comfortable with. At some point in their early life, when dependency was a necessity, there was a failure in their primary carer's capacity to adequately meet those needs. In severe cases this could cause malnutrition or marasmus and even death. That is very unlikely these days, although failed dependency seems not to be, if my practice is a guide. These unfortunate people yearn for a relationship with another - they have an attachment hunger in which the attachment is more important than its quality. However, they choose people who from the point of view of an outside observer are incapable of allowing dependency and in most cases I have come across are actually counter dependent; that is they are actually terrified of dependency in themselves and are unable to let anyone in. They seem unavailable and remote and their behaviour is unreliable. They are constantly late, break commitments and rarely see anything wrong in their treatment of their partner. One could be forgiven for thinking that under the circumstances, the dependent one would run for the hills. But they do precisely the opposite. The more let down they are, the more attached they become. One might also think that the unavailable one would detach and leave the dependent one and in fact this usually happens when it can do the most damage. In the meantime however, the dependent one fills a powerful need for the counter-dependent one. He or she actually contains the other's denied dependency. "It's not my problem, it's his/hers!" It is not difficult to imagine the strategies employed by the needy one. S/he escalates all the behaviour available to draw the unreliable one closer and with predictable effects, creates more distance.

In all these simple cases, and many more, there is a deeper understanding that can and must be reached if we are to free people from their compulsive madness - repeating the same experiment in the belief that it will turn out differently. It is as if we are all stuck in groundhog day; endlessly repeating "self and other" destructive patterns of behaviour and believing that the world - the object - is making us do it. The fact is that we write our own lives with the tools we were given as children and in the end WHAT WE GOT IS WHAT WE WANTED even when it seemed the last thing we wanted. The trouble is that the "last" thing we want is usually the last thing we get.

In the hope that this is sufficient for the reader to understand the Mad Hypothesis, I will now elaborate my development of the model as I presently use it in my practice. This will be a simple elaboration without the details which the book will fill in, but hopefully enough to enable a basic grasp of the idea.

The Three Level Model of The Mad Hypothesis.

> LEVEL 1
> *The Desired Object - Also referred to as the Absent or Lost Object and sometimes as the Absent and Lost Object*
>
> LEVEL 2
> *The Real Object or Present Object*
>
> LEVEL 3
> *The Feared Object*

▨ The Desired/Absent Object.

The desired object is simply whatever it is that the person believes would cure her of her distress if she possessed it. This can be money, a better job, a car, a husband who loves her, more affection, friendships, peace of mind. Its fundamental quality is that it is missing, lost or absent. This object provides the main motivation for all human activity, apart from the mundane life maintenance activities one does to survive. Its absence is felt to be the main reason for the constant or repetitive feelings or experiences of distress that most of us suffer from, whether this is fear, anxiety, sadness, shame, envy, depression, jealousy, spite, anger, rage, loneliness, disgust, rejection, abandonment, failure, unworthiness, loss, self-hatred, poverty, wrath, greed, lust, etc. If asked, a person can usually articulate what would make them feel better or ease the chronic distress - the absent/lost object. This can be difficult if the absent object is "peace of mind" as that is what most people yearn for, in the end. The difficulty is that the person is describing a relationship with an absent self and it can be hard to reduce its absence to "stuff" in the outside world, particularly where their distress is a result of childhood abuse and lifelong depression.

The Real or Present Object

This describes the person's actual life situation with respect to the absent or lost desired object. Of course there can be, and usually is, more than one desired object. It can be money and a good partner, for example. The desired object arises from the person's actual present experience of their life with respect to the feelings of distress mentioned above. We live in a state of fairly constant emotional distress unless we are distracted or close to possessing the desired object. Anxiety is very common of course and most people feel it often. It is hard-wired. We are evolved to feel anxious. It makes survival of the species more likely - an unpalatable thought! As I said above, the desired object can be anything, either concrete or abstract, and most people spend most of their lives acutely aware of the gap or gaps between the present object/s and the desired/absent object/s. The attainment of the desired object becomes a motivating force for activity unless despair or passivity (depression) sets in after too many experiences of failure to achieve it. The crucial element is the gap/s between the desired object and the real or present object. That absence is felt to be the reason for the chronic distress. The solution to the distress is obvious - get the object or change the present one so that it stops being absent and becomes the desired one - for example, change your partner's, boss's, children's behaviour, get the job you covet or aspire to, have as much sex as you want, win the lottery, finish the PhD, write and publish books, become a celebrity, get on TV, etc.

It is relatively easy to see (or elicit) that the feelings of distress connected with the real object have been the person's experience of living for so long as she can remember.

▓ The Feared Object

At the risk of being coy, I will save elaboration of this object until a later point, and after I have illustrated the part played in everyday life by the desired and present objects.

For the moment let me simply say that this is the object that we all spend all our lives trying to avoid. It is an internal object, not one in the 'real' world, though it is more powerful than almost any object one might encounter out "there". The feared object is the real origin of the default settings. It is truly frightening for anyone who is not secure or genuinely contented - at least forty per cent of the human race. It is actually a "repressed" part or parts of the self and usually involves unmetabolised feelings and "forgotten" memories.

▓ The Relationship between the Present and the Desired (absent) Object

The most important thing to say about the present object and the chronic feelings of distress it engenders is that those distressing feelings are the human equivalent of the default settings on a computer. They are the feelings to which we always return when the going gets rough, and most people can identify that they have felt this way for as long as they can remember. One problem is that most people don't know what the roots are of the feelings of distress, at least consciously - they know the feelings are very familiar and in the universal state of repetitive madness they believe they are caused by present circumstances. In other words, by the failure of the real object to meet the standards of the desired and absent object. What then is the solution to our graduate human psychologists' problem?

Simple. Do what we have always done before. Change the present object for a new one or change the behaviour of the present object to the fantasised and yearned-for standard of the desired/absent object. It matters not that this experiment has been attempted a hundred or a thousand groundhog times before. If it didn't work it was simply because s/he didn't do enough of it or do it with sufficient intensity or diligence or gusto. So just do more of it! The pursuit of the desired object can then begin in earnest; AGAIN.

This is where people begin to get really interesting. It's also where relationships with objects become fascinating. The experiment (like buying more lottery tickets) is, like all the other trials, doomed to failure. It doesn't matter how many times you throw an apple in the air, it will always fall to the ground. Which is fine if you want to demonstrate that Newton was right, but not when you believe that finding another partner who will not neglect you will mean ending up with a partner who does not neglect you. The problem with a default setting of feeling neglected or unwanted is that, as with all other default settings, you have an investment in being neglected! In other words, you are experimenting to fail. If you are a sportswoman or an ambitious corporate executive, you are competing to fail. This takes us back to the question of my bewildered patient: "are you saying that I want this distress, this pain and suffering?"

I'm afraid the answer is yes. The whole idea of the experiment, unconsciously, is to end up with the default settings, whatever the conscious intention. This raises the question of the "gap" between the real and the desired/ absent object and, precisely, what is the function of this gap? Let me first say that this gap is where at least forty per cent of the human race spends most of its thinking time - or at least what most of us believe to be "thinking". Actually it is not thinking at all. It is really time spent in planning dramas, working over old dramas, or feeling distress about dramas - failed experiments. The gap between the desired and real object is where the insecure amongst us live for most of our lives. I hesitate to ask, but who amongst us is not insecure to a varying degree? Even the most secure of us has painful default settings which sound a clarion call when the going gets rough. Which of us does not carry a painful past, however little of our memory banks it occupies?

However, intellectually, this is where the going gets rough. Why should anyone want to end up with the default settings - the distress - after the experiment is complete? Why should anyone want the distress? The answer to this is that of course we don't want the distress (although this raises the question of masochism and I will address this later). In fact, there is a genuine belief and conscious wish that the experiment will and should succeed. However, we are thwarted in our conscious intentions by the intentions of our unconscious. The default settings are just that, they are almost hard-wired in terms of social learning. It's hard to believe they are biologically hard-wired although some recent neurological research may indicate that they are. The problem lies in the belief that the default distress is caused by the failure of the real/present object to live up to the standard of the absent/desired object. Nothing could be further from the truth unless someone is holding a gun to your head or you are suffering from real and tissue/psychologically damaging abuse; and even if you are suffering abuse you may have unconscious motives for being in such a dangerous situation with a vicious and threatening or damaging object.

At this point I want to return to Dean's story from the last chapter:

We can see what I came to call the "absent/desired object" very clearly. He had a strategy for changing the present object (his wife), to which the default settings (feelings) were attached, into the desired object, the woman he thought he wanted. This is the drama and the script; the strategy is the behaviour he employed to achieve his "consciously desired" outcome. What of level three, the feared object? This was the necessity for him to face the original abandoning and rejecting adored mother with whom he had undoubtedly had a very close relationship prior to being sent away to school. The grief, rage and fear that this experience held was overwhelming as is every early trauma for everyone. The defaults are in place to hold it at bay whilst simultaneously offering the hope of finally doing away with it through the "drama". The problem is that the drama gives both primary and secondary gains. The main primary gain is that he never had to take the risk of real intimacy and real love. To do so would threaten his childhood position of never risking being hurt again by a woman he loved. His fundamental world view was maintained and his psychological economy was stable. He avoided the unbearable pain of being sent away. The secondary gains were many, the foremost being that he had a ready-to-hand explanation for why he was unhappy - it was her! The next chapter will explain Dean's behaviour much more clearly.

This takes me to the point of the use of the gap and its functions in a person's everyday life. Effectively, the gap (between the present object and the desired object), as I have said, is where most insecure people (and everyone else when they are feeling temporarily insecure) spend most of their time in the internal world.

This activity in the internal world (which most people call "thinking") is focussed on how to make the present object into the desired and absent object or how to possess the desired object. In order to achieve this, where secure people set realistic goals and make realistic plans to achieve them, insecure people indulge in drama to achieve unrealistic goals. This raises the next crucial question which the next chapter addresses. What do I mean by drama and what is its function?

3

The Function of Drama

Freud was frustrated and perplexed by the problem of passivity and placed himself in all manner of theoretically difficult positions in his attempt to explain its contradictions. Basically, passivity is a problem with doing things. I can recall vividly my own analysis with David Malan when I, and he, suffered greatly with a complete unwillingness on my part actually to do anything. Most of the time I felt as though there was nothing I wanted to do but, interestingly, I did not feel at all depressed. His consistent content interpretation was that I was struggling with a conflict between doing things for myself and my unwillingness to do things for my parents, in particular my mother, because I believed she had given me so little that I did not feel I had enough internal resources to spare to devote to doing other things. A subsidiary interpretation concerned my sulking and going on strike to punish her by withholding, as she had withheld from me. Of course the process interpretations of the transference (the patient confusing the therapist with a real figure from her life or past and having the same thoughts and feelings towards him) and counter-transference (the therapist's feelings towards the patient - hopefully generated by the patient and not the therapist confusing the patient with someone else from her own life) were the most important by far. Why did I want him to fail and feel frustrated even if it meant the possible failure of my analysis? Could it be that I was as angry with him as with my mother and wanted him to experience the frustration I had been made to feel as a child? Was I sulking with him? In his normal way, he presented these interpretations as questions rather than as certainties and encountered all the resistance you would expect from someone in such a state of mind. Incidentally, I have never held to the view that the transference should always be made explicit. If an interpretation is made about any relationship I believe it is always understood unconsciously that the same is being said about the analytic or therapeutic relationship. As far as possible I try to limit my explicit transference interpretations to those occasions when the transference is clearly functioning in the service of, or as a resistance to, treatment and this is not always easy to judge.

Developmentally I have come to see passivity as being concerned with a child's initial conflicts with mobility, whether to crawl or walk and also with anally-derived conflicts about giving and taking – demands – originating in the experience of maternal demands for toilet training. I am not unaware that control and mastery are also at the heart of this problem. Fundamentally I believe the child feels he has not been given enough to have sufficient left over to give to his mother. Clearly there are serious attachment difficulties here and one sees them repeated in the transference.

Passivity is highly conflicted for men and much less so for women. Doing nothing is the antithesis of masculinity which is primarily defined by activity or doing. As I have already said (Is There a Cure for Masculinity), masculinity is what men do – it is not some essential internal state which is easily differentiated from femininity. This is why external markers are so essential in defining and managing the "essential" difference – the presence or absence of penis and breasts. Passivity is associated with femininity and unconsciously with castration and impotence and powerlessness. In the construction made famous by Freud, passivity is associated with masochism and femininity, and activity is associated with sadism and masculinity. It is a cliché that when a woman discusses a problem with a man the first thing he wants to do is solve it. Unfortunately this is not her aim. She wishes to air her thoughts, discover what she thinks and get closer to him. It is a cliché, but nonetheless worth repeating, that women are more interested in processes and are content to view reality as emergent whereas men like to fix reality and want events with beginnings and ends and are inclined to want to end processes as quickly as possible.

As we grow up we all learn to be intolerant of uncertainty – not knowing, being lost, are feminine – and are not given to reflection, characteristics which make us very unfitted for dealing with internal conflict and anxiety. As men, we are educated, raised (wired) for action and activity. This is no less so when it comes to dealing with internal conflicts. I want to explain how passivity (a universal capacity) affects the ways in which people handle these difficult internal events. Of course it is not without importance that uncertainty evokes existential anxiety as it taps into everyone's greatest fear, death.

Since its inception, psychoanalysis has been preoccupied with the question of masochism. Any therapist who maintains a secure practice, in which people form a strong attachment and stay for some years, will have been repeatedly impressed with the observation that many of us repeat acts or patterns of behaviour and continue to do things which are painful or self-harming. I mean this in the most ordinary of ways rather than what might be called the extreme self-harming of slashing or cutting or indulging in life threatening sports/ sexual practices or addictions. These activities are what I call drama. In this chapter I want to examine the meaning and function of drama and the importance of dealing with it in therapeutic practice.

Freud made a famous distinction between the primary and secondary gains that people get from being ill. Secondary gains are obvious ones like attention, success, affection, having no demands made on one, etc., and primary gains are concerned with the maintenance of psychological stability and security, however fragile. In the context of my three level model, secondary gains are the ones achieved by pursuing level 1 and primary gains are those that derive from maintaining the psychological stability of staying in the default position - level 2 - however uncomfortable that may be. Although I have never found it useful in explicating primary processes, Transactional Analysis (TA), as developed by Eric Berne, has always impressed me with its clarity and power in understanding and explaining secondary gains.

For those of you who are not familiar with it I should explain the basis of TA. Berne took Freud's concepts of the superego, ego and id and renamed them, respectively, Parent – Adult – Child. With this simple device (which, for these purposes, I have made simpler than it is in both theory and practice) he was able to do what psychoanalysis has never been able to do: to analyse and describe the everyday social transactions which manifest neurosis and other forms of pathology as well as normal, non-pathological relationships. It also provided, as Bateman, Brown and Pedder pointed out, a powerful tool for understanding some elements of transference and counter-transference in the analytic encounter. In a major departure from Freud, Berne assumed that each ego state (as he called his trilogy) was capable of communicating with any and all of the ego states of any other person and that this could be done consciously. In other words we are all capable of behaving as parent, adult or child in relation to others and of doing so in a conscious attempt to reach a particular ego state in them. Further, each ego state is capable of unconscious communication beneath the conscious or manifest one. Each communication can therefore consist of both latent and manifest elements and be aimed at eliciting particular responses from a particular ego state or combination of ego states in the object of the communication. Berne called the unit of communication a "transaction".

Diagram Ego States

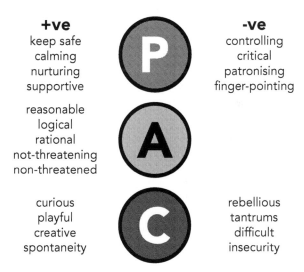

+ve
keep safe
calming
nurturing
supportive

reasonable
logical
rational
not-threatening
non-threatened

curious
playful
creative
spontaneity

-ve
controlling
critical
patronising
finger-pointing

rebellious
tantrums
difficult
insecurity

Figure 1a: Ego states and a transaction

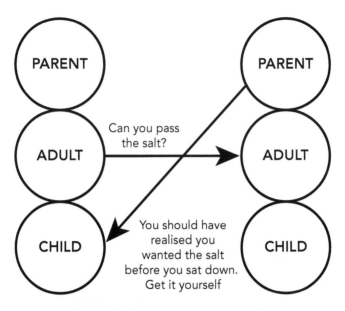

Figure 1b: Ego states and a transaction

For example, the adult to adult request, "Will you put your coffee cup in the dishwasher" can be heard as a parent to child statement, "You don't do enough around here" (see Figure 1). Of course it may also contain this latent message. The response completes the transaction, and may be similarly loaded with latent content. In fact, it is difficult to say anything that does not have latent content. When we combine these units of behaviour – transactions – with another element of TA, the "Drama Triangle" (Figure 2), we have available a powerful tool for the analysis of drama and acting out in the lives of both individuals and groups.

VICTIM
"I'm Blameless"
Safe – "Love me no matter what"

Drama - Crisis
Energy

What's your favourite role?
Consuming

The Karpman Drama Triangle

RESCUER
"I'm Good"
Accepted
Enabling Role –
Indifference is an
important tool.

PERSECUTOR
"I'm Right"
Power

Figure 2: Drama Triangle Diagram

Stephen Karpman, who devised the triangle, opined that every drama involves the actors assuming one of the roles on the triangle and that each person has both a favourite role and the role which it is being used to defend against, but in which the person inevitably ends up at the conclusion of the game or drama.

In Berne's theory, we see the first systematic account of the role of drama in people's lives, as well as the tools for understanding it. These tools possess a face validity and explanatory power which the analytic concepts of "repetition compulsion", "return of the repressed", primary and secondary gains and "acting out" simply cannot match (although the gains are undeniably matched in what they lose to subtlety). Although Berne and modern transactional analysts would insist that TA is an equally powerful tool for understanding primary gains it is truly an analysis of secondary gains. In the simplest terms, TA sees games, what I would call drama, as being dedicated to the maintenance of the status quo, both socially and psychologically. In other words, people's aim is to keep relationships, and the external world, the same as they are and have always been and to prevent disruption in their way of seeing and being in the world, even when these might both be painful. It is the human equivalent of the "default setting" on your home computer and level 2 in my model. These defaults are not always known to the person - indeed few of us have insight although people often ask "why do I always do that?"

To some, this is a definition of masochism. The difficulty with this explanation of the origin and motivations of drama is that it depends on an understanding of latent transactions, which is not so far from the Freudian notion of the unconscious; it is in the unconscious that the desire to maintain a painful status quo is held and from which dramatic behaviour is driven. What then is drama? In psychoanalytic terms I mean by it what I would mean by the term "acting out". Laplanche and Pontalis's explanation of Freud's definition (insofar as it is of interest here) is as follows:

"Action in which the subject, in the grip of his unconscious wishes and phantasies, relives these in the present with a sensation of immediacy which is heightened by his refusal to recognize their source and their repetitive character."

I have to say that I use a fairly broad definition of acting out in that I see it as the acting out of transferential impulses AND the substitution of action for remembering. For me it includes many forms of behaviour which are employed to avoid anxiety and internal conflict evoked by the work of analysis or therapy instead of working on the anxiety or conflict in the analytic process. However, I do not see all forms of acting out as being the result of analytic transference. In fact, in everyday life, "acting out" is the normal dramas which people compulsively repeat in their relationships, and it has the same aims, the avoidance and management of anxiety and the maintenance of the social and psychological status quo. The objective of the analytic process (from a very old-fashioned point of view) is to bring everything into the transference (the relationship with the therapist or analyst) and in this case every acting out, even when it is a repetition of behaviour long pre-dating the analysis, would be seen as an expression of acting out of the transference. I prefer to think of acting out as the enacting of any impulsive or compulsive behaviour in everyday life, whether or not it is linked to the transference. Personally I am gratified when a piece of repetitive dramatic behaviour, which compels the person into treatment, gives way to therapeutic work even if it is related only to the past and/or its present players and not the transference. I realise that my working definition conflates the compulsion to repeat, the return of the repressed, and acting out in the formal sense. Although this might lack intellectual rigour, it provides a basis for useful therapeutic intervention which provides more efficacy and satisfaction than rigour.

In terms of TA (and for me psychoanalysis), drama occurs when someone repeatedly falls into one of the roles on the triangle and attempts to manoeuvre others into complementary roles. So a victim needs either a persecutor and/or a rescuer. A rescuer always needs a victim and a persecutor to rescue them from, and a persecutor always needs a victim. The point about these roles is that they are not simply one-offs, adapted at a whim, but they are life positions which we all (according to the theory) adopt, at least those of us who are not gifted with psychological health.

Drama fulfils a number of very important functions in our lives. From the point of view of the unconscious I believe its main function is to validate and legitimise certain beliefs or core constructs about the self and others and the world in general. It also functions to provide the possibility of converting trauma into triumph by setting up re-enactments of familiar painful events in the hope that this time the outcome will be different. Let me give an example which I come across often in my practice. It concerns men, though just as often women, rescuers, who continually choose relationships with others who are damaged or distressed, victims. They take on the task of relieving their companion of distress and depression. What is striking is that the victim never loses their distress and remains a suffering victim. The rescuer, meanwhile, becomes increasingly resentful that all his efforts are to no avail and his rescuing position slowly mutates to that of internal victim and external persecutor. He begins to believe that she is deliberately refusing to get well, or happy or whatever it is she is supposed to do in his script. He feels that she is persecuting him. What this man is trying to do is relieve his mother of her depression so that she can begin to do what she was always supposed to do – take care of him. Unfortunately, his unconscious attachment to a neglecting, depressed and needy mother is profound. In order to relate to a woman in a different way he would have to abandon his internal mother to her fate – something which is beyond him. The fear this evokes cannot be underestimated. Fundamentally it is the fear of death, for that is the fate of an infant who is without a primary carer. So long as she exists and is needy there is always the possibility of salvation for the child. A man who rescues - or indeed a woman - needs to ensure the continued existence of the victim who needs rescuing! This is easily achieved by subtle forms of persecution masquerading as rescuing or providing help, behaviour which is designed to perpetuate dependency, helplessness and a need to be rescued.

I have always had my own understanding of drama, culled from years of reading and talking to patients who do it. It involves the idea of the projection of roles. In Kleinian theory the act of forcing another to take on a dramatic role would be called projective identification. For example, the writer of the script – the author or patient – experiences states of distress (level 2) resulting from unconscious persecution by internal objects (feared objects, as we shall see). This persecution can be an actual attack of a humiliating, sadistic kind (in fact quite appallingly cruel) or it can be the experience of being neglected or ignored – in both cases these are continuations of early childhood or infantile experience. In non-neurotic people (and after all the differences are quantitative not qualitative – we are all fairly close to madness much of the time whether or not we know it) the outcome of this internal persecution will be experienced as inexplicable mood swings or anxieties of a sort common to us all. Usually we are not aware of the attack itself (although self-reproach is common and this can be one manifestation of it), but only of the emotional outcome. Invariably this will involve a form of anxiety which may be associated with an unpleasant feeling about the self or others.

We are all relatively powerless in the face of our internal world and primitive identifications and internalisations. How do we fight back? Who do we fight? Explicitly paranoid people can project the persecuting voices into others and fight or fly from them. In the case of psychosis the voices are "heard" as if they come from outside – so there is an illusion. The psychotic believes the illusion and is therefore "deluded". For most of us the voice remains inside the head, if we hear it at all. Or we have a fantasy that the other person is "thinking" something about us, such as that we are stupid or "bad" in some undefined way. I will elaborate what this badness is later. If the voices or persecutors remain internal we cannot fight them. Our responses are limited to containing the distress, seeking support to get us through a temporarily difficult time or seeking recourse to a fix – mind-altering substances such as shopping, drugs, food, alcohol, medication, masturbation, sex, pornography, risk-taking behaviour (all part of the dramatic script), etc.

There is one other alternative which can be employed in conjunction with all the above: that is drama. If by some means we can employ another to take up the role of the internal persecutor or the failing/absent lost object (even if we only imagine they are doing it) then we have someone we can actually fight back against or otherwise influence to change in the desired way! It is impossible to overestimate the psychological benefits this offers. If we can fight it or change it we can beat it and beating it means an end to the lifelong internal persecution/neglect/shame/scorn etc. that we have endured. If we cannot beat it we can denigrate it or otherwise reduce its status or stature in the world. If this is successful then, in effect, we dis-empower it and this is as good as a defeat and, in fantasy, signals the end of the default settings. Naturally, there are certain difficulties involved in any of these processes and outcomes. The first and most obvious is that these dramatics are taking place with real people in our lives. In certain states of madness it can be entirely in the realm of fantasy, as with a love affair with a star or the hatred of a public figure. As one wag put it after the demise of Richard Nixon, repeated after Mrs Thatcher met a similar fate, "Who are we going to hate now?" The problem with real people is that they have a habit of having minds of their own and plans and dramas of their own. This can make for very unpredictable outcomes of one's dramas, or at least apparently unpredictable. The failure of the drama is only an apparent one - unconsciously it is the failed outcome that is actually being sought. In the drama, one has to become more and more hostile to defend against or deny the variables which are not under one's control. Actually none of them are under control and that is the essence of the dramatic story. I should clarify that 'hostile' in this context means an increasing disavowal or denial of the reality of the object in favour of an escalation of the fantasy that they will change if I apply more of my dramatic moves and strategies.

These dramas are the stuff of everyday life for most people. If our own lives lack drama we apparently tune in to TV soap operas in our millions in order to keep the level of dramatic arousal to its required level! A fairly common drama, and one with which I am very familiar in my work with people in relationships, concerns the fantasy that someone close to us does not like us or is in some other way feeling antipathy or malice towards us. This will be based on the experience (not necessarily the reality) of being disrespected in some way and feeling shamed or humiliated (the infamous male "sense of injustice" – the origin of the equally infamous "male paranoia" and the equally famous female feeling of being neglected or not being desired and wanted). This can be precipitated by the most innocuous of stimuli which would go unnoticed even by someone else present. It can be based on no more than a fantasy, and on an act undone rather than committed. The man will quickly fall into a feeling that he has been unjustly treated and will begin an argument designed to right the wrong or get redress or vengeance. Equally often he may fall into a sulk and withdraw in a fuming, hurt rage. Feeling like a victim of an injustice, he feels more than justified in persecuting the perpetrator of it. He will continue to persecute until he feels that injustice has been equalised. Such dramas can end in death or serious physical harm to others.

Although the behaviour of disrespected abusive men and unhappy victimised women is over-determined from a therapeutic viewpoint, it is transparently obvious to me, after working with many such people, that they are all projecting onto their partners an internal persecuting female object or a rejecting male object, almost certainly their mother or father, and a very early one at that. It is not by any means necessary that she should have been actually persecuting in a physical way. I have said in earlier books that one might have to begin to account for many extreme projections by including in any lexicon of early trauma the mother who is not attuned to the infant and whose mirroring of her is faulty or deficient. The consequences of a lack of attunement, in my opinion, are potentially disastrous. An infant can be adequately serviced and simultaneously have her selfhood, or potential selfhood, negated. She can end up carrying an indigestible object which she experiences as negating her existence, of inflicting a narcissistic wound of overwhelming import. She simply cannot contain the object or the pain it inflicts (this also affords the opportunity to backwardly project the pain and fear entailed by the beginning of the Oedipus complex). By projecting firstly the neglecting, and secondly the persecuting phallic mother into the current partner she temporarily rids herself of a poisonous internal object, and the pain she causes, and simultaneously gives herself the opportunity of fighting back.

Another drama, which I have also come across enough times for it not to be seen as an especially deviant one, concerns men and, less often, women, who organise sexual games involving another man or woman with them and their partner, either as voyeurs or participants. The variety I have heard more often is the one in which the husband invites another woman to have sex with him and his wife. The other variety is that in which another man is invited into the relationship. It is hard to say which is the more risky or dangerous and they are both certainly that! Stoller has said often that the most exciting sex is sex that carries the greatest degree of risk. The difficulty is managing the risk so that the excitement does not fall over into danger. Psychoanalytically, the drama involving two women is the most disturbed, although the one involving another man is the most dangerous. Either way, these dramas rarely end well.

Robert Hinchelwood has spoken about the role of drama in hospital communities and groups within those communities.[4] Stoller has written at length about the function of drama – particularly sexual drama and perversion in maintaining psychic health and disease.[5] Although they both write for different reasons and from different perspectives, their analyses are similar. In essence they conclude that the main motivation for drama is the management of trauma or painful experience or troubling aspects of the self. They all involve the projection of central aspects of each into other people. At first sight it is hard to understand why someone would want to be involved in watching or taking part in sexual activities with their partner and another person, especially given the potentially destructive intensity of jealousy in intimate relationships. This ought to be the case whether the "stranger" is a man or a woman. I have worked with many men who produce this particular dramatic triangle.

A particularly severe one involved a man who used to do it only when he had taken large amounts of cocaine, a substance to which he was seriously addicted. His drama was transparent. He would encourage his partner to take cocaine and then to go out with him and pick up men with whom she could have sex whilst he watched. On only one occasion, surprisingly, did the man also penetrate him, something which he withheld from me for some years. These episodes would always end with him having sex with his partner and he was quite clear that he was attempting to prove that he was the better man – at least consciously. The underlying trauma he was attempting to master is clear, (proving himself to be a better man than his father or, more rarely, a brother) as is the fact that it did not work or it would not have been necessary to repeat the drama often. In addition, this drama was actually a subsidiary one.

The drama does not always require people to be major players. A favourite non-object relation drama (at least concretely) is the relationship with money. The story I am about to recount has links with much else that I will say in this book and I will return to it. It concerns a very wealthy man - let us call him Colin - who was obsessed with his income and his accumulated wealth. He occupied much time every day in calculations of his "net worth", usually in the context of his anxiety that if he were to drop dead his family would have sufficient to take care of them for the rest of their lives. It should come as no surprise to learn that this man worked in the City in a very highly paid and responsible job in global finance (now much maligned and not always fairly). His annual salary was the equivalent of most people's lifetime earnings. He is, quite simply, very rich.

Sadly, Colin was also very unhappy and anxious and filled with undifferentiated rage towards others which he was afraid he would act out. He sought me out for treatment for this homicidal rage (which he had never acted out, even mildly) although it quickly became obvious that he wanted to resolve his anxiety and his depressive sadness. His depression gave way quite quickly. However, what emerged was a high level of basic insecurity and anxiety about his survival. He actually had no faith in his own 'going on being', his continued existence beyond the present moment. He functioned as if his life were about to end in death or some other catastrophe. Of course, it was not difficult to make the connection between his earlier depression and his fear of death and catastrophe. The depression we had initially seen had been a mere shadow of itself and as we gradually pieced together his history we began to see its origins in his very early childhood and to understand that he had been depressed since about the age of five and it had gone unnoticed.

His anxiety about his survival was expressed in a conviction that he was going to lose all his money or that all his investments would collapse and he would be poverty stricken. I could not overstate the strength of his conviction that this was imminent and most of his waking life was devoted to making as much money as he possibly could (level 1: the absent/desired object, money). Of course, it was impossible to reassure him that this was not about to happen (particularly if you had suffered the stock market crash of 2000!). This anxiety, although relatively easy to analyse and understand, proved almost intractably resistant to change; whenever he was under any sort of stress, internal or external, he would resort to calculating his net worth or calculating new ways of increasing his wealth. Mammon, the need and greed, held him in its thrall.

Its final defeat in the therapeutic process seems to me to illustrate many of the really important things we need to understand about drama. Let me outline the problem as we came to understand it. Even though we worked this problem through many times in treatment and had developed a good understanding of its roots and meaning, Colin seemed unable to stop his calculations or his anxiety about his wealth - level 2. What became apparent was that he conflated his net asset value or worth with his value as a human being. Whilst sitting in his first class plane seat he would look around at the other passengers and attempt to calculate their net worth against his own. He felt that he was a fraud and that, in situations where he was with people who were worth more than him, his deception would be unmasked and he would be seen for the conman he really was (2). Of course, his perception that his fundamental value was contingent on his personal wealth is not particularly odd. Society (maybe even biology) has a vested interest in maintaining that conflation. The most obvious thing to say about Colin's anxiety is that it concerns loss and, moreover, loss of a catastrophic nature (the feared object - level 3). Next, it seems clear that, barring a major calamity which would affect most of humankind, he is unlikely to lose all his money or the assets in which it is invested. Additionally, it mattered not how much money he owned. In fact it seemed that the more he earned and owned the more severe his anxiety became. In part this is not so hard to understand, given that the more he owned the greater he stood to lose, although this was not the cause for his increased anxiety - that was more connected to profound guilt about having anything of value when he felt so valueless (and particularly when the salaries paid to bankers are so ridiculous).

Whenever he acquired a large amount of money he would raise the bar on the amount he needed in order to feel secure (level 1). He understood that the reason he wanted so much was that he was profoundly insecure. He believed that this insecurity was financial and therefore that the solution to it was to have as much money as possible and with it would come financial security (he would have the absent/desired object: level 1). Apart from the fact that this is impossible to achieve absolutely (as J.P. Getty said, 'you can never have enough'), it was clear that the insecurity could not possibly be financial. As his wealth increased by leaps and bounds and his insecurity and anxiety persisted (level 2) he did what most of us do when presented with a difficult problem – if our solution is not working we believe that we are not doing enough of it. He concluded that he did not yet have enough money to feel secure and that what was needed was more of it (level 1). Colin's nose was pressed to the grindstone in a big way.

We gradually began to understand that the resistance to giving up the fantasy of total security through financial wealth was that in this way there was at least the possibility – or the fantasy – of solving or defeating the problem. It originated in the outside world and its solution was in the outside world. The reality, which we began to appreciate, was that it existed in his inner world and there it felt to him, unconsciously, to be insoluble (the feared object: 3). The catastrophic loss (3) he feared was the loss of all internal worth or value, and ultimately his capacity to love, a capacity about which he harboured serious and frightening doubts. The loss of all his wealth was a metaphor for the emptiness/poverty of a part of his internal world which he struggled to suppress, repress and deny. The fear of external catastrophic loss was a metaphor for going crazy; for him, we came to understand, this would mean a terrifying, debilitating depression (3)].

I have always been a fan of Winnicott's dictum that "the breakdown you fear is the breakdown you have already had".

For "breakdown" one can substitute any trauma. Of course one cannot hold to this too rigidly but it is, at times, a useful enough clinical or life guide. Any unresolved trauma can be projected forward and dramatised if it provides the illusory possibility of resolution. Freud observed that most defence was against the idea of one's mortality and eventual death, although I believe that this is something most people really only appreciate on reaching what Arundati Roy called the "viable dieable" age (around early old age or later middle age). Then it becomes an idea with which one has to grapple on a regular basis. Death is too far off for the young to be concerned with – if one ought ever to be concerned with it. What are the origins of this anxiety? Is there a universal anxiety about death, an awareness which we carry from the moment of birth? Or is this existential anxiety instead a response to early loss or similar experience which attacks the fundamental nature of attachment? In other words, is it a response to trauma? The difficulty for me is that I have never seen anyone who did not seem to have been traumatised even where it was impossible to determine precisely the nature of the trauma. It could be said that my sample is a self-selected and, by definition, unrepresentative one. However, I do not think it would be going too far to say that it seems we are all victims now as the moral panic about the dangers to children has reached epidemic proportions. There were circumstances and events in his early life which adequately explain Colin's condition and his preoccupation with money even without adding social conditioning into the mix.

Not that there was a single epiphany. There were many on the route to his loosening his grip on the obsession with money and wealth and each was as important as the others. Gradually, as his depression gave way to the underlying rage and guilt and finally to the underlying fear and sadness, he became more and more at ease and able to appreciate and enjoy the wealth he had in his family and friendships.

There is another drama, so widespread as to require special mention. It is in the nature of my practice that I see a great many people who are having "relationship difficulties". Almost invariably they present as a victim of their partner. The nature of the victimisation varies in the expression but the variation is usually only on the more general theme – my wife/partner is persecuting, neglectful, depriving, promiscuous, frigid, or not good enough in myriad ways, which leave the person feeling angry, afraid and sad. More often than not, my patients are acting outside the relationship in ways that, if they were not secret, would end the relationship.

Let me give an example. It concerns a man who was referred because he had pushed his wife away from the doorway when she was attempting to prevent him leaving the house to spend the evening with his friends. She had been mildly hurt and had called the police. She refused to press charges so he was not arrested, but he was escorted from the house and did in fact spend the evening with friends. She really could not win in this situation! He spent a long time recounting the history of their marriage and how she had always been like this. She did not like him socialising with his friends and always complained when he did so. There were two children from the marriage, aged eight and three. He was a softly spoken, small man who I could not imagine being violent or threatening. He did disclose however that he could get very angry with her when she attempted to stop him going out. He insisted that he did not act this out with her other than to raise his voice. He was adamant that he never threatened, insulted her or demeaned her. In response to my question as to when this drama had started, he told me that it had begun when their second child was born. It quickly emerged that he had always gone out to see friends and smoke cannabis. In fact he had been doing this as often as three, and sometimes four, evenings a week since they were married. Prior to the birth she had questioned his behavior, but the intensity of this questioning, and the demands that he change, increased markedly afterwards. His resentment and anger and feelings of victimisation had increased proportionately. His self-presentation as a passive, mild mannered and softly spoken man stood in sharp counterpoint to his description of his wife as an angry harridan whose behaviour was unreasonable and at times quite mad. It was not difficult to feel some sympathy for his plight. He had always been a good provider and, when he was at home, an involved and caring father. This had been confirmed by a third party involved in the referral who was at a loss to unscramble the relationship's problems.

It is hard, too, to convey the depths of this man's distress at his plight. He simply could not understand why she was so angry with him for wanting to spend a little time with his friends.

I have deliberately chosen a relatively mild example (and I could as easily present her side, as I am sure the reader can) to illustrate men's victimisation at the hands, and particularly mouths, of their partners and the powerlessness they all report in the face of the 'attacks'. I could multiply this a hundredfold. What I intend to do is account for men's construction of these unreasonable harridans with whom they have chosen, apparently mistakenly, to have children and spend their lives. I am interested not only in their motivation for constructing such dramas of persecution and victimisation but also the methods they use. Sometimes the subtlety is admirable.

This man's feelings of resentment and confusion at his wife's treatment of him served many purposes and, as we unravelled them, it became clear that he was as much, if not more, the author of her behaviour as she was. In particular, it rapidly emerged that there was no intimacy in the relationship and had not been since the birth of the first child. He dated the onset of the real difficulties, when she started 'attacking him', as he put it, to the second birth. However it was obvious that he had been struggling since she became pregnant the first time. His trips to see his friends had been a way of withdrawing from her and protecting her from his growing resentment at his demotion down the feeding chain in the family. He was required to give more as he was receiving less and he was unable to do so without resentment and anger. It was not difficult to see that he was in a serious sulk. The point is that however much he protested the lack of intimacy in the relationship and her responsibility for it, it might have been designed to maintain his psychological stability. In brief, like many men, he did not want intimacy with his wife and, more importantly, had never wanted it! What he required was control, and the significant thing about the control he required was that it would enable him to have the sort of intimacy he wanted *when* he wanted it and on his terms and in his time. It requires little reflection to see that this does not meet any of the requirements of intimacy in a relationship. Intimacy is the antithesis of control. It requires vulnerability, openness, and disclosure in order to allow one's personal and self-boundaries to be crossed without threat and anxiety – highly feminising.

He constantly provoked her (level 1) with taunts that she was a bad wife (level 2) for scolding him and suggested that if she stopped he might want to spend more time with her. Of course, if she stopped, he did not change his behaviour and the cycle continued. Pathologising her need for intimacy (the pursuing wife) shifts the focus of concern away from its more legitimate target, the man. By setting up this drama in which she becomes the bad object who has to be avoided or changed (level 1), justifiably, he never has to face his own anxieties about intimacy and what it is that really frightens him and that he runs away from (level 3). The "distancer" husband is fundamentally afraid of women – perhaps all men are. The secondary gains from his drama are clear. He gets to see his friends as often as he wishes and to feel guilt-free about it. He gets to avoid all the onerous duties associated with being a father and running a home and having a marriage. The primary gain is fundamental. He never has to face his real anxieties about being close to a woman. This is as clear an example as could be of how to maintain a default setting, unhappy, unloved and hard done by, by attempting to change the present object (level 2) into the absent object (level 1) yet doing it in such a way that it is self-defeating and yet affords substantial secondary gains.

Another common example is the sibling of the distancer – the frigid wife. She is usually to be found with the distancer, as sexual intimacy is simply another, but in some ways more threatening, form of contact when engaged in with a long-term partner. The issue is the same. She needs to have sex, but it has to be on her terms and in her time and place. Failing that, she is an undesirable, unwanted and ugly woman ('castrating bitch' in his terms) and obviously he doesn't want to have sex with her. It may be true that she is not interested in the sort of sex that interests him. More than likely, she would like some sort of emotional intimacy as a forerunner to genital contact – some sexual intimacy rather than simply fucking.

Lest I be thought sexist here, let me say that I know that women also sometimes like to just fuck. In an intimate relationship I like to think that this is possible, and that a man who is not intimacy-phobic will be happy to follow her agenda just as she is happy, at times, to follow his. The truth is that many men I have worked with are reduced to impotence by a woman wanting sex. It is simply not feminine for a woman to want to be in control of, or at least to share control of, a couple's sexual relationship. As women will say, in so many words, they have never had a sex life of their own, they have always had their partner's sex life. Sex occurs when he wants it, where he wants it and how he wants it. The strategies men use to maintain their control are not always subtle, and repetitive drama plays a large part.

I recall one man who would always create a reason to never go to bed at the same time as his partner so that she would always be asleep when he eventually did so. He had already established sufficient control that he had managed to define the bed as the only location in which sex could happen, in spite of her many protests. Often he would manage to provoke a minor disagreement so that the relationship was frosty late at night. I could multiply the strategies many times but suffice to say they all served the same purpose. Whenever a man tells me that he does not have as much sex as he wishes because of his partner's sexual problems, I now automatically make the silent interpretation that he is afraid of sexual intimacy. I make the same interpretation to the frigid wife but, naturally, I do not articulate this without some preparation.

I hope I have said enough about drama and its motivations to enable the reader to see beneath the manifest content and to have confidence in her understanding of her plight. In treatment, sooner or later, the difficulties will be enacted in the transference. All it requires is patience. My thoughts about drama and the way people dramatise in relationships has led me, over the years, to develop a particular way of intervening which I have found useful in situations where the space between a couple is so full of mad projections that any form of reality-testing or analytic reflection seems impossible. That is what I have referred to as the Mad Hypothesis and which then evolved into the 3 level model with which I began this book.

What follows is a detailed description of a relationship in which the wife was in treatment with me for five years. I use it in order to illustrate the difference between dealing with the Mad Hypothesis and the default positions, not only in the interests of the reader but also in order to demonstrate how I work in clinical practice. Some of the ideas I present are theoretical but with very clear practical application for anyone reading this book. Whilst I will name the theory, I will present it in such a way that I hope the reader will see how she can apply it to her own life and dramas.

Rebecca and Robert. A "successful" drama

Robert is a highly successful entrepreneur in his early thirties. He has been previously married - a marriage which failed, he initially believed, because his wife wanted children and he was not ready to interrupt his developing career - a career which turned out as well as he had hoped. Of course he did not love his wife as much as he, or she, had hoped and the divorce turned out to suit them both. It had always been a volatile relationship involving a lot of arguing and temporary separations, not always, though often, occasioned by his work commitments. What his ex-wife did not know, and what had brought him to see me, was the secret life he had led and which had steered, inexorably, his new relationship into serious trouble. He recognised that there were similarities between the trouble in this relationship and his marriage but he was unable to articulate the similarities, apart from the arguments and the volatility, or the underlying issues. In fact, the underlying issue - the secret life - did not emerge in his treatment for a year, so ashamed was he of his behaviour. I have no intention of going into the details of this secret life or the psychological origins. Suffice to say that he is a rare man with a deep interest in many fetishes and fetishistic sex, which neither his wife nor his present partner knew anything about.

His major complaint was that his partner insisted on "arguing with him". Now, apart from the obvious, that arguing is an interaction, it quickly became clear that one result of these conflicts was his increasing resentment, which, once it had reached a pitch, would propel him into a secret sexual liaison, guilt-free because the conflict between them meant they rarely made love. He was utterly unable to see how he actually generated the arguments either strategically, by being emotionally unavailable, or tactically by articulating criticisms of his partner which he knew from experience would upset her deeply.

It was not difficult to get him to accept the intellectual insight that he was generating the conflicts, and to see the similarity with his failed marriage. Having him accept emotional responsibility took somewhat longer. This was a simple application of the Mad Hypothesis and his acceptance that the way he ended up feeling was as familiar as consciousness itself. At this stage I was unaware of his secret life so our work to establish the underlying dynamics was obviously delayed. The default position - at least the major one - is apparent. He was chronically disappointed and sexually dissatisfied with his partners and felt unloved and unwanted. I do not want to elaborate the origins of his sexual perversity, which was essentially sado-masochistic, but the feeling of being unloved and unwanted was not difficult to trace back to his lifelong feeling that his mother had never loved him enough, although it was clear that he had treated her like a princess. It is worth pointing out that his relationships with women were emotionally sado-masochistic.

On a lighter note, my siblings and I used to be amused by the way our father often generated minor squabbles almost every Sunday morning so that he could go to the club and share a drink with his friends. He could simply have asked Mother and she would have been happy to give her approval but this would not have obviated his guilt.

It is important to stress that one of the main functions of all drama - in the gap - is the maintenance of emotional stability and the reinforcement and legitimisation of a world view, and that this world view gives meaning to living - it provides purpose. It also supports the unconscious world view and legitimises it. Finally, it offers hope that this time the drama will be resolved in a way that the default settings will dissolve and peace of mind will finally be achieved. I hope I have given sufficient examples of the nature of drama and how it serves to maintain that psychological stability - however unstable or unhappy the person may feel.

There is another question to take up here, and it concerns the role of drama in the psychotherapeutic process, a process which proves necessary when the person is unable to resolve the defaults and the accompanying dramas without external help. Before I take up that theme, it seems time to explain what exactly the feared object is.

4

The Feared Object

Rather than enter into a long theoretical discussion about it, I will describe the therapy of a young man who finally dealt with his most feared object. It needs to be stressed that this object, always a person from earlier life, is an internal one. I know this can sound rather strange to people who are not familiar with the idea of an internal world, although its existence is not so difficult to demonstrate, as the chapter on anxiety will have shown. Taken to extremes, it is not difficult to imagine an internal parallel world running alongside the familiar world of consciousness. Even in the conscious mind we are all familiar with holding conversations with internal objects, although most people would describe these conversations as fantasies. We have arguments with our partners, make love with familiars, or strangers we have seen. We talk to the boss about a pay rise or our performance, or his, and so on. Much conscious activity consists of these dramas or ordinary events being played out in the mind, and we are aware of them; some psychologists call this fantasy life "thinking" or "planning". It is much harder to imagine that we may also be doing the same thing in the subconscious and unconscious mind, almost as if there is a separate person functioning inside us. I describe these processes because the feared object is one such, and entirely unconscious.

However, it is not very difficult for a trained observer or a very aware reflecting person to become aware of the unconscious through inference, and access to dreams (what Freud called the "royal road to the unconscious") is not the only route. The content of the unconscious can be inferred by observing behaviour which seems contradictory, or hard to explain consciously, or where we are at a loss to know what motivates us to do things that lead to undesirable or unwanted consequences when we could, with a little thought, have predicted those consequences.

There are many simple examples from everyday life and I imagine most of us could think of our own. For example, passively disobeying our boss's instructions and being disciplined for it, treating someone badly and being hurt when they retaliate, using addictive or mind-altering substances, having illicit sexual liaisons, getting angry with authority figures, habitually being late, etc. In many of these instances it is not hard to trace those behaviours back to early patterns of relationships with important people in our childhood or much younger life, often with surprising effects on the behaviour!

The young man I will describe had a long-standing repetitive pattern of getting into relationships with women and, after a short time, usually a few days, rejecting them passively. He would not tell them, he would simply not contact them and would ignore their attempts to communicate. He had done this with hundreds of women over a long period starting in his teens. He came to me because he had finally met someone whom he could not reject, although she was very concerned about his treatment of her which involved frequent bouts of anger and withdrawal and many disagreements about small and seemingly unimportant things, mostly initiated by him.

After about a year they had finally gone to see a couples therapist who considered that the problem was the man's and who, knowing of my work, consulted me. I hasten to add that this man was not a violent abuser and, in fact, most of his behaviour would be considered normal by a large proportion of men. By this time his partner had started saying that she was finding it very hard to stay with him because there was so little calm in the relationship. It was obvious that it was hanging by a thread. He also told me that he often thought of leaving her, even though he stressed that he loved her very much, as she loved him.

It was clear to me that his behaviour could easily be explained by the coherence test of truth with regard to his previous pattern of seduction and rejection. The difference was that he was now acting it out with the same woman rather than a series. I suggested this to him during his assessment, tentatively, and he immediately picked it up and ran with it. This boded well for his capacity to use a talking dynamic treatment and we agreed to work together. During the early months of our work, he was having a lot of success in changing his behaviour insofar as the acting out, the anger, the arguing, etc were concerned. However, his tendency to withdraw gained pace as a defence against the desire to act out. He was fully aware of this yet felt unable, as yet, to stop. It had emerged early on that this very bright and confident man had never felt any grief about any of the relationships he had broken, nor had he ever regretted what he had done, or losing any of the women.

Soon, things spiralled out of control for him. His partner told him, unequivocally, that she needed to take a break to think things through. Initially he had agreed to this with some relief. However, within days he had begun calling her to arrange to meet. He mailed, wrote, texted and called, all to no avail. In fact she eventually told him, after a couple of weeks, that she had decided to end the relationship completely. What happened was not a surprise to me. I had concluded early on that he was unable to tolerate rejection and that his behaviour was probably driven by a need to punish women and to stay in control of his emotional life, to which any commitment represented a substantial threat. To put it bluntly, he collapsed into one of the most regressive and frightening states of grief I had ever witnessed. He had strong wishes to die to stop the pain yet he was also terrified he was going to die. He was unable to function at work, ate from memory rather than hunger, and spent a great deal of his time crying and wailing like a baby. I have to disclose that I was also afraid for him and often thought his treatment was not sufficient to contain him.

I referred him to a psychiatrist colleague who prescribed anti-depressants. After a little these did begin to help insofar as they seemed to take the edge off his profound anguish, although the feelings remained conscious. I cannot begin to describe the intensity of his feelings of loss. Somehow, describing his fears of death from loss, cannot convey the depths of his pain. He said he had "lost everything", "nothing means anything anymore", "there is no point in living without her", "life is unbearable". These things, and many more, he re-iterated frequently in every session. By this point it was clear to me what had happened, although analysis was having no effect on his emotional state. During the times in his sessions when he was not emotionally overwhelmed, he was able to agree that his state was not to do with the loss of the relationship. He loved her and he knew that his breakdown was precipitated by her rejection of him but also that it had evoked something in him that was not related to her. The question was - What?

I had frequently taken him into his memories of his mother and the quality of his relationship with her. He was profoundly protective of her and would bridle if there was even a hint of criticism in anything I said. I had obviously pointed this out and he had readily agreed. He said they were very close. The father was still alive, though had been absent for much of his life and the marriage was not a good one. The father travelled a great deal and when he was at home the marriage was volatile and there was a lot of arguing and shouting - hardly surprising. He loved his father but did not like him.

What was obvious to me was that at some time in his early life he had felt deeply rejected by his mother and may even have experienced a time of abandonment by her when he did not have the cognitive or emotional capacities to process what was happening, certainly before he was two or, more likely, one year old. There is no doubt that his conscious memories of his mother, and his description of his present relationship with her, were accurate. However, it also became clear that he had indeed suffered a prolonged separation from her during his first year when she had tired of her husband's treatment of her following the birth and had become quite deeply depressed and required hospitalisation on a number of occasions. During that time he had been cared for by his grandparents. That absent and "internal mother" was his feared object. I need not describe the course of his treatment from that point on. Suffice to say that he did eventually emerge from his regressive breakdown, more appropriately described as a "breakthrough".

During the remainder of his time with me he did not cease to miss his ex-girlfriend although the pain was substantially mitigated. His feelings towards her are a good example of "transference" where we relate to a person as if they are someone else. Unconsciously, she was his mother and was the first woman he had stayed with long enough for that transference to occur. Why she should be the first one to receive that transference is another question though a large part was played by the fact that she resembled his mother in so many ways, physically and emotionally. It should come as no surprise that separations from me during long holidays were extremely difficult for him and that it was during the analysis of his transference to me, as his mother, that he formed his first long relationship and precipitated his eventual breakdown. Looked at through this lens, his previous behaviour fell into a system of meaning which was entirely rational. It became clear why he needed to repeatedly seduce and reject women and inflict such pain on them. Of course it was self-protective but, unconsciously, it expressed a straightforward revenge motive and enabled him to project into those women all of his deeply repressed feelings of loss and rejection. They felt it, not him.

What were his default settings and his present and desired object? Prior to his treatment, he had been a young man playing the field and having a good time with his friends. He was emotionally unattached to anyone outside his immediate family and had never attached to a potential partner. His default setting was detachment and being in control. He had always wished he could find a permanent partner but never with any intensity, as his behaviour indicated. His feared object, the rejecting mother whose absence was life-threatening, is also obvious and was deeply unconscious. His present object was an absent one, the woman he wished for, whom he could find and stay with. However, her absence was a direct consequence of his rejecting behaviour.

He wished for a present object but, as is clear, his fear of the real absent object and his need to be in control of her absence, dominated his behaviour.

Lest it be thought that the feared object is always the "mother", I will give an account of a woman whose feared object was her father. She was a mother of four children when she first came to me. She was a very wealthy, half owner of a business started by her husband. Most of her time had been spent looking after her children, who were now almost grown up and on the verge of leaving home. She was very dissatisfied with her life and wanted to change it but was very unsure of the direction she wished to take. It became clear that the main source of her unhappiness was her marriage. She came from a culture in which women occupied a submissive, secondary status and were expected to always do their husband's bidding. Surprisingly, she had not seen any of this. She had accepted that this was the norm in her culture and all her friends, from the same culture, were the same as her. She felt guilty that she was miserable when she had so much compared to others. It was very difficult for her to articulate her complaints about her husband and it took many months of painstaking work to enable her to face her denied feelings about him and her marriage. She was aware that she had always wanted him to be different but had put this down to her lack of gratitude for his hard work - he was a workaholic who was mostly away from home and in his office till all hours.

I did see her husband once, at his request and with his wife's permission. He was a very clever, charming man but was extremely controlling during our meeting. I saw little point in challenging him as it was clear, even during our short chat, that he had some serious personality problems and that his childhood had been troubled. His wife, my patient, was frankly one of the most guilt-laden people I had ever met and it was clear that he missed few opportunities to exploit and potentiate this. I used to tease her that she felt guilty about every bad thing that happened in the world. I thought it was best to be light-hearted about it lest she end up feeling reproached about feeling guilty.

It should be clear what her present object and desired object were. Her default settings are also clear. She was approaching the awareness that she did not feel loved by her husband and that she actually believed he did not love her. We had analysed her childhood quite extensively and her relationship with her father was the mirror image of her relationship with her husband. He had been a workaholic, always absent from the home. He was a distant and authoritarian figure and she had no memories of ever having received affection from him. Her attachment to her mother was secure and loving and had remained so. Although it was clear to me how she maintained her default settings of unhappiness and loneliness in her marriage, it would be some time before she was able to start to unpack this or even accept that it was the way she wanted it to be. She gradually began to accept that her father had never shown her any love and that she believed he did not love her. As she began to metabolise this, her grief about it began to emerge and with it her sadness about all her unrequited love for him. She became deeply and truly bereft for many months. Unsurprisingly, she had not felt any grief when her father died. Now she began to mourn the father she had never had. As her father was now dead there was no opportunity for any real reparation, only acceptance.

It was at this point that we began to seriously examine how she made her husband behave in the way her father had with her. She began to see how she was withdrawn and sulking with him and how she was easily angered with him and passive-aggressive in response. She recognised that this was how she had behaved in response to her father but she clearly had no responsibility for her father's affectionless distance from her. Her whole life she had carried the unexpressed grief and sadness about the failure of that relationship and this was the underpinning of her chronic and conscious unhappiness.

She stayed in treatment for some time and began gradually to change her behaviour towards her husband. She also become more assertive and able to articulate her feelings rather than act them out. She was more contented with her life and herself and was developing clear ideas about the life she wanted after the children had finally flown the nest. As I have always maintained, if you want to change your partner, change yourself. It matters not where you intervene in a system. A change in any element of it requires that the system change. It was no different in their marriage. Her husband underwent radical changes in response to hers and the relationship became more secure and intimate. Of course, it was not without difficulties. All marriages are difficult. That is not problematic, but how we deal with those difficulties more than often is.

I hope these case histories illustrate the nature of the feared object and why it is feared. It is always unconscious, and keeping it so is the motivation behind the drama, the stuff, constructed in the gap between the present and the desired/absent object. I read recently that happy people have no past whereas unhappy people have only the past. It's nonsense of course, but it does contain a kernel of truth. We are all victims of our past now and our identity is our past. Who are we if we have no memory?

We now have what I hope are clear descriptions of the default settings and their relationship with the three different levels of my model.

5

Drama and the Therapeutic Process

I think this is an appropriate point to describe the role played by the default settings and the present and absent/desired object in the therapeutic setting.

When it proves impossible, in spite of all efforts, for the patient to separate the "stuff" from the default settings and the drama proves too compelling or too subtle to deconstruct, it is time to consider outside professional help from a well-trained psychotherapist. Generally speaking it is not a good idea to source such a person from the internet. Recommendations from friends are usually reliable. If google is the only resource than I advise seeing at least two or three people before selecting someone to work with. Although such meetings are fraught with anxiety, it is important to check their qualifications. Any therapist or analyst worth their salt will have no difficulty in being straightforward in confirming their training and experience. If they make a comment about your having a problem with trust before doing so, then I recommend you do not see them!

I also recommend finding someone who does not work too far away from your home or place of work. Psychotherapy is demanding in many ways and it can be difficult to re-arrange your life to fit in with regular sessions. Most practitioners will offer to see you at the same time or times each week and are usually willing to negotiate fees. Do negotiate! This may be a long-term commitment over some years and those few pounds less can amount to a lot of money. Also, expect to be told that, if you miss sessions, you will be required to pay for them, although most therapists offer some flexibility in well defined circumstances. If all goes well, you are about to enter what may turn out to be the most important relationship you have ever had, so be prepared. Naturally, I cannot say what will happen to you in the process but it is possible to outline how the default settings, the stuff and drama, will enter the therapeutic process. To do this I will draw on the ideas of David Malan, a renowned therapist and psychoanalyst.

Malan used a couple of very simple diagrams to explain how drama comes into the therapeutic person. They are both triangles:

TRIANGLE OF PERSONS

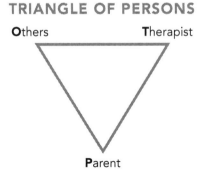

Others   **T**herapist

Parent

Figure 3a: The triangle of persons

TRIANGLE OF CONFLICTS

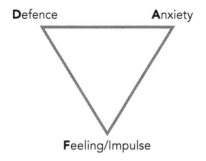

Defence   Anxiety

Feeling/Impulse

Figure 3b: The triangle of conflict

The triangles are standing on their points because Malan wanted to emphasise that there is a direction of movement downwards from newer to older material and relationships, with the unconscious impulse or feeling emerging last and hopefully with the realisation that it is related to the original figure, in most cases the parent or feared object

What these two diagrams illustrate are the processes that occur in psychotherapy. However, Malan unpacks what I refer to as "stuff" into two separate elements, the hidden feeling underneath the anxiety which drives the drama, and the people involved in the drama. As you will already know, I prefer the term "object" to "person" as I think the drama can involve any element in your life which you want to change and think will help you to reach a peace of mind and the final defeat of the stressful "default" setting.

Therapists of an analytic persuasion, who follow Freud in whatever particular school - and there are quite a few - all attempt to do the same basic things: to make the unconscious conscious and to bring the patient's material, stuff, into the transference. In the terms of Malan's triangle of person, this means that the therapist understands, whether or not he or she says it, that everything the patient/person says about stuff in his life, whether it is work or people, is also a comment to the therapist about their relationship. The theory is quite simple. Firstly, it is more than likely true but the patient does not know it. The communication is unconscious. Secondly, it is easier to resolve conflicts when they concern the person you are actually with, and they can be understood and discussed or interpreted in a way which enables resolution. It is important to understand that when a person enters into psychotherapeutic treatment they automatically regress to earlier stages of development. It is almost as if they are hypnotised. They will not be aware of the regression but they will be aware that their anxiety increases in the presence of the therapist. It is not hard to imagine. Most people get anxious when they meet a psychotherapist socially and wonder if he or she can see deep into them. It can be unnerving. It is rather like meeting a hypnotist socially. People can become anxious that they are being hypnotised without knowing it and will be made to do something out of character! Thirdly, it is an axiom of analytic theory that unconscious conflicts are not truly resolved unless they have been resolved in the transference - that is, in the relationship with the therapist or analyst. It must be remembered that the therapist represents every important person in the patient's life, especially the parents. At first this is not conscious, but it can quickly become so. It follows therefore that any unresolved issues with the parents will in effect be resolved with them in the process of resolving the transference. Remember, that is the theory and the practice is not always so smooth or so effective.

What this means in practice is that the patient/person will involve the therapist in every drama she describes with people outside the treatment. If the therapist is good enough he or she will stay one step ahead and see the drama coming. I hesitate to say it, but this is not always true. The only way to avoid ever getting involved in a drama is to stay completely silent - often the only strategy if the therapist is inexperienced and/or uncertain. Notwithstanding that, it needs to be said that we are allowed to be wrong and it is crucial to be able to disclose this and then work with the consequences. A parent's most important work in helping their children to mature is often done through failure. Also, this is the only way for the therapist to know what it is like to be a person/object in the patient's life. We have to be able to step into the river with the fear that we may go under, yet be confident that, when necessary, we can get back to the riverbank. People know this of course and will do all they can to sink us even when they know it will not be in their interest. However, they need to know that we can survive the worst they can throw at us. Our job is to survive! Fortunately, most of us do, most of the time. There is the very real question of what the therapist does when they become the feared object, which they must become in order to help their fellow travellers/patients, to reach psychic contentment. That is a subject for another book. Suffice to say that we need to be able to tolerate being feared and hated. Unless we can do so, we cannot help the patient to tolerate those experiences.

6

Anxiety and the Unconscious

Everybody is nowadays familiar with the word unconscious and the fact that we are all supposed to have one. Its existence can be demonstrated with reference to what Freud called the "psychopathology of everyday life". In the book of the same name he illustrated, with examples such as "forgetting" and "slips of the tongue", that we can no longer take for granted that our conscious mind is in control of events within our minds or, indeed, our behaviour. A music teacher friend provided me with a humorous example of a slip of the tongue which betrayed what she could not say out loud. She said to a difficult pupil "shall we try some shite reading?"

Freud was not the first writer to make use of the term "unconscious". It had been used by many others long before he expanded and universalised it. At the start it was a shocking notion and not only because of the qualities with which Freud endowed it. Even today, the construct cannot claim consensual status except within the psychoanalytic profession. There are respectable non-psychoanalytic therapists who have great difficulty with the idea of a structured, reified unconscious as Freud described it.

Freud's ideas are now well known. They have been widely disseminated and most people are familiar with the idea that our conscious self is not necessarily in control of our behaviour, feelings or thoughts. Nonetheless, there are still many unresolved logical and semantic difficulties with the idea, even though it is generally accepted as a daily demonstrable fact of life that much of what we do, think, and feel cannot be understood by reference to what is readily available in conscious functioning. It will be very hard for anyone to practise dynamic psychotherapy without some conceptual understanding of why this is so. Of course we are all familiar, and comfortable, with the idea of unconscious material. We all of us know that there is a great deal of knowledge and information which we know, and know that we know, and which can be called up when needed but which is not in consciousness. It is like a hard disk which we can access as necessary when we need the information it contains. This hard disk has the primary quality of unconsciousness; it is out of awareness but is more what we might call sub-consciousness. There is another sort of unconscious material, however, which is not accessible at will. This material is actually being kept unconscious. It is material which we do not want to know and do not know we know. Psychotherapists call this not wanting to know "resistance" and the process by which we hide material "defences". For example, the fable of the fox who decided that the grapes were sour after he had tried, in vain, to reach them on the vine illustrates one way of rationalising (the defence) failure – and keeping the pain at bay.

There are major differences in the way these two types of information are processed in the mind. The readily available hard drive obeys all the rules of formal thinking. It is logical, it is reality tested, it is linear in time and causality, it is not internally contradictory – we do not think that A, which is opposite to B, is true when we also believe B to be true. These rules, which are essential for everyday living, are known as the rules of "secondary process". We all learn them with our acquisition of language and they are employed, for most of the time, by the conscious "self".

The second type of unconscious material – which we resist knowing and actively "unknow" – obeys quite a different set of rules: the rules of "primary process". This part of the mind is almost a separate person inside all of us – a structurally separate part. It has a life of its own in which people and information are treated without regard for secondary process rules. Contradictions abound. Mutually exclusive truths coexist. Time is at a standstill, causality is not linear, information is not reality tested, internal reality rules. Something is true because we believe it to be true. Although there may be long periods when the conscious mind is the victor and has established hegemony, this victory is never finalised. It is a battle which has to be fought over and over again. The healthier we are (from one point of view) the longer will consciousness be dominated by secondary process, but any of us can be overwhelmed at any time and primary processes can achieve dominance over our functioning – as in compulsions, depression, phobias or morbid feelings. These distinctions, and the existence of the two parts of the self, are not always so clear in our minds. At one extreme is mental illness in which the conscious mind is overwhelmed by unconscious material. To an external observer this can be quite bewildering, particularly if one is talking to a floridly psychotic person in whom delusions and hallucinations alternate with moments of lucidity. Although in a less extreme way, even most ordinary people will have experienced similar processes at times in their lives. In states of jealousy, for example, we are all capable of thinking the most appalling thoughts and having frightening impulses about someone we love. This temporary insanity seems bizarre when we later recover our equilibrium. Perhaps even more common are states of grief or mourning that can seem, to the sufferer, so similar to states of pathological depression - grief is a normal form of madness. Normally optimistic and robust dispositions can be overcome by feelings of loss and despair, bordering on the suicidal.

One of the most common signs of the imminent danger of a breach of the boundary between our unconscious and conscious selves is anxiety – we all experience anxiety. A simple example mentioned earlier and observable in every psychotherapeutic/counselling practice, is the increasing anxiety felt by many patients as breaks in treatment loom closer. They will report the anxiety but are often completely unable to accept any interpretation which connects it to the upcoming break. The reasons for this are multiple and resistance to its interpretation is particularly observable in male patients in my experience. Female patients seem to take more readily to the idea that they may be sufficiently attached to a therapist and feel abandoned by him. Usually it is not worthwhile making an interpretation until it has happened a few times, and then only a gentle suggestion is called for. Plunging interpretations are usually resisted. In this case the threat is of loss and the anxiety is separation anxiety – probably the most debilitating and painful of all forms of anxiety. The loss is both the imminent one and, more importantly, the much older and unmetabolised experiences of loss, the denial of which is essential for the patient to maintain her functioning.

Anxiety does not always imply the danger of an incursion of the unconscious into the conscious self – clearly there are many realistic sources of anxiety. These, however, can be employed by the unconscious and cause an excessively anxious response to quite ordinary sources of worry. This happens when an everyday event evokes in the unconscious mind echoes of situations which seem similar. All events are processed by the unconscious. The barrier works, in the main, in one direction only: from the unconscious to the conscious. The unconscious mind is animal, primitive, infantile, and dominated by passions. If it were to overwhelm the conscious self, normal functioning would be impossible. Anxiety is a signal that this might occur, and that the conscious self had better take avoiding action. Everything contains the potential for evoking primitive responses from us. Clearly, however, some of us are better defended than others against this possibility. What makes this so is an important question insofar as it is probably a major determinant of the extremity and intensity of a person's "ordinary deviance" and the extent to which their behaviour is synchronous with their self-image.

There are simple, everyday examples of the unconscious which most people experience and about which Freud wrote very amusingly in *The Psychopathology of Everyday Life*. Ordinary examples include forgetting, slips of the tongue, misreadings, mistakes or errors, etc. How many of us have not had the experience of saying something only to realise that we have used a word the direct opposite of the one we intended to use?

Compulsive or addictive behaviours are illustrative of unconscious conflict. Smoking when we know that it might kill us is one such behaviour. Most people will do something which they don't like or which causes them anxiety and yet they feel unable to stop it even though it conflicts with their value system or their morals or their self-image. They feel powerless in the face of the impulse. Such situations would not exist unless there were a part of the self which was not accessible to consciousness. Identity is not seamless. We all live with constant conflict.

In part, this is because of another fundamental difference between the conscious and unconscious minds. Apart from the unconscious being dominated by primary (non-rational) processes, it is also essentially animalistic and is governed by the "pleasure" principle, whereas the conscious mind is governed by the "reality" principle. The unconscious seeks nothing more than gratification of the impulse, whatever it may be. It is without conscience or values or morality. Under the influence of the pleasure principle, in which pain is avoided and satisfaction is sought, unconscious ideas, feelings, impulses, and processes strive for expression in consciousness. The "primary process" is basic. It is older than the "secondary process". Its objective is simple: gratification/satisfaction. Thinking, which is a secondary process, is inhibited action. It is not difficult to see why the conscious self should be in conflict with the unconscious when its only concern is gratification.

The function of consciousness is to negotiate with reality and organise our lives to satisfy as much of our unconscious wishes as is possible and is commensurate with maintaining our membership of the community. Naturally, this does not apply to people who are suffering from mental illness and are overwhelmed with anxiety or with the primary process. Obviously, secondary processes have survival value or would never have developed. Healthy individuals learn to be satisfied with achieving a compromise between the demands of reality and the demand for gratification. My patients fail in the task to differing degrees and, to the extent that they fail, develop symptoms. In general they come for psychotherapy because they want the symptoms removed. It is a common fantasy that there is a psychological equivalent to surgical removal. It is a source of disappointment when they learn that this is fallacious and that they cannot simply hand over the symptom as if it were an illness and I were a physician - it is impossible to "cure" someone of being themselves.

Anyone practising psychotherapy without placing the unconscious at the centre of their endeavours is not practising dynamic or analytic psychotherapy. For the reader to understand what follows he or she needs to accept its existence without question although its nature is open to debate and disagreement.

7

Stopping the Drama

How to stop Pushing and start Pulling

I am frequently asked by my patients what they need to do to stop dramatising and reinforcing the default settings attached to the Present Object. Leaving aside the necessity of detaching the default settings from the events, the stuff to which they "get attached", discussed earlier, I usually end up having a conversation about the difference between "pushing" and "pulling". Almost invariably, when we try to make the other person/s in the drama act out the role/s which we have assigned to them, we have to use subtle and not-so-subtle forms of manipulation (usually forms of "projective identification" in which we actually make people feel a certain way, often without knowing we are doing it) to get them to feel, think, and behave in the way that will enable us to achieve the outcome we "want" (the pain of having the default reinforced). This is what I call pushing.

To give a simple example, which every parent will relate to, your child is having difficulty sleeping and keeps coming to you and asking for comfort. Psychoanalytically, there can be many reasons for this but it is much easier to treat it as a behaviour problem involving the child's need to control. A standard parental strategy, apart from comforting and reassuring the child, is to cajole or bribe it to go back to bed. This is all well and good, but if it continues for any length of time this behaviour becomes distressing for both parent and child. Paradoxical interventions - doing the opposite of what seems natural - can be very effective in such situations. For example, waking the child up before it normally does so spontaneously and then keeping it awake will soon lead to pleas to be allowed to go back to bed and sleep. Believe me when I say that in the majority of cases this will need to be repeated only a couple of times to stop the child waking up. This is an example of "pulling". I realise that this might seem cruel to many parents, but I have seen it used sufficient times to be confident of its efficacy and its kindness.

More appropriately, let me describe how "pulling" compares to "pushing" in the everyday, default-re-enforcing dramas that occur in the chronic unresolved painful conflict that some people take for "marriage". I am thinking of the reverse situation of what is usually referred to in marital therapy literature as the "pursuer wife/distancer husband" syndrome. That is the situation is which the woman is constantly bemoaning her husband's emotional and physical distance from her and her chronic feelings of loneliness and deprivations. She pushes for more intimacy and/or reproaches him for his behavior, and the more she does, the more he uses her (nagging) behaviour as a justification for withdrawal, and he usually pathologises her need for intimacy as over-neediness or neurosis. The literature less often describes the reverse of this situation, the pursuer husband/distancer wife, but this is also common. Detached/avoidant attachment disorder is not confined to men!

Men I have worked with in this situation almost always describe a mother who was distant and unemotional and from whom they never received sufficient love or affection. This establishes the default setting for later life and the outlines of the drama for maintaining it - he pushes for intimacy, sexual or otherwise, and gets rejected and feels chronically unhappy, insecure, needy, and deprived.

For the sake of clarity, let me add that this memory of the rejecting mother is just that - a memory. I do not invariably assume that it was a reality. As I have written elsewhere, men have many motives for constructing a "rejecting mother" and she is the origin of woman-blaming in every man who does so (see *Why Men Hate Women. Jukes. A.E*).

So we know how he "pushes" until he gives up in despair or dysphoria. "Pulling" will be very difficult for him as it involves giving up the habits of a lifetime. First he has to stop "pushing" and this involves accepting that he is married to a woman who is unaffectionate and ungenerous (actually someone whom he has created as unaffectionate and ungenerous through both subtle and unsubtle means). What he's got is what he wanted! It is utterly pointless for him to attempt to create the absent/desired object from the formed pot of the present object. I realise that this also means that he has to come to terms with the possibility of outcomes that will be very painful for him if his contribution to the relationship system is dramatically changed. The notion of "system" is very important here. All systems have multiple points of change. If I want to change the temperature in a room I can do this in many ways. Whichever way I choose, the whole system will have to adapt to my choice. So it is in relationships, or dramas.

In this, as in all cases, stopping the drama means isolating and separating the pain of the default setting from the person whose behaviour is being blamed for causing it. I call this behaviour the "stuff". I do not underestimate how difficult this is to achieve in practice and nor should the reader. It can take many failures but each attempt will get you closer in the end.

For the "pre-occupied/ambivalent" man to change his drama of trying to change his "dismissive/avoidant" partner into the desired object, he has to give up the attempts to change her. He can do this only by accepting that she is avoidant and that the more he attempts to get close to her, the more she will avoid and reproach him. In other words, he has to leave her alone and, without sulking, maintain a consistent, loving, and accepting manner. To say that this is difficult is an understatement. He also has needs and she does not meet them. What he normally does, makes it even less likely that his needs will be met. In the end, if he gives up his drama, which inevitably involves his punishing her for her frustrating behaviour, he may decide that he has to break the relationship. Apart from any practical difficulties such as children, housing, finances etc., there is the much more difficult problem of his facing his feared object - the mother who did not love him or did not love him enough.

I cannot count the number of men and women I have coached in ways of becoming obscure with dismissive/avoidant/fearful partners. The avoidant partner gains great reassurance from having a constantly needy partner who is pushing for more intimacy. The best way for the pushy (preoccupied) partner to "pull" is to become more avoidant. This is pulling but it means changing so many habitual forms of behaviour which are designed to get back, again, to the default settings - rejected, lonely, unhappy, anxious, needy, etc. Accepting that those habitual behaviours are designed to perpetuate the problem is very painful but not nearly as painful as abjuring them. It is unfortunate that becoming more obscure also means staying in the game of these very painful sexual politics insofar as it is simply an attempt to shift to a different end of the continuum. It is, however, possible to become obscure without being in the game and without staying on the continuum. This involves dealing with the transference onto the avoidant partner of the relationship with the earlier and much more powerful object, the mother or the father. This is so much more easily said than done, as anyone who has attended a group for co-dependents (a misleading name for the condition it describes, in my opinion) will testify.

In the end, learning to pull means having the courage to face the feared object. Whether it is in romantic relationships, work or career, the feared object has to be faced in order for us to be free of our past. When the desired/absent object is a person it is relatively easy to diagnose the behaviour problem that leads us back to the default setting, the present/frustrating object. This may be a boss or a co-worker, a wife or a close friend. It is so much more difficult when the desired object is an abstraction such as money, or academic success. Often, dealing with the feared object involved in an abstract/desired object means facing one's limitations. We are not clever enough, talented enough or handsome enough, or we simply lack the energy required to achieve the desired object. Facing one's limitations is a painful experience but, in the end, reality is more reassuring than fantasy.

The important first step is to identify the pain - the default - and the presumed cause of it - the absent/desired object. Having done that we then need to identify what it is that we are doing to change the present person (object) into the desired object. This is hard work because it involves giving up the habits of a lifetime. It calls for reflection, not action, and reflection is a skill we, mostly, have not developed. So much of our behaviour is habitual. We do it without thought and it is mostly anxiety-driven so giving it up involves having the courage to face anxiety and distress. If the drama involves the most important attachment in our life then the anxiety may be severe as this attachment echoes back to the first life-giving/preserving ones - the parents. The default settings then have to be experienced for what they are - a major part of ourselves and omnipresent. Giving up the drama means letting go of the hope that we can change those first attachments into what we wished they had been - a futile but, nonetheless, equilibrial and life-sustaining hope. We are as we were created by those attachments and, existentially, there is nothing we can do about those events, notwithstanding the statement "it is never too late to have a happy childhood" which, to some extent, we believe. The point is that the present attachment is a recreation of the original attachment. We all project onto our current relationships aspects of the early ones, and the more important the current relationship is then the more primitive and older are the projections. Romantic attachments recreate relationships with parents as care-givers, friendships those with siblings or school friends, and authority relationships those with mothers, fathers, and teachers - but this is a special case and I will address it in a separate chapter.

Detaching the default feelings from the other person/object in the drama and giving up pushing represents the only hope that the other will change their behaviour. A change is inevitable; if any element in a system changes then the whole system has to adjust in order to maintain equilibrium. So the person/object will change but it may not be in the desired direction. However, for the reader, the choice is between persevering with the experimental madness and committing to chronic default disease or taking the risk of changing with the possibility of finding some default-free peace with the present person or with someone else in future.

To recap: pushing is what we do to get the person involved in our drama to change and become more like we think we want them to be. So if we are not getting enough we demand more and reproach them for depriving us. They are demanding so we complain about their selfishness or nagging. They are quiet and distant so we press them to talk. They don't want to be involved in something which gives us pleasure and we keep pressuring them to be so. All pushing is when we try to change someone's behaviour to suit our needs or wants and there are myriad strategies for this. At best it leads to short-term compliance when it is accompanied by threats or punishment. At worst it leads to the behaviour we want to change becoming more entrenched and the strengthening of the resistance.

It is worth taking a little while and asking yourself about the difficult areas in your life and looking at them through the prism of the default settings, the present object, and the absent/desired object. As I have said, the "object" need not be a person, it may also be an abstraction, a career, money or your aspirations. If you are stuck in a repetitive pattern of behaviour intended to achieve a goal which it fails to achieve, you need to see it for what it is and change your behaviour or give up the goal. I realise this is easier said than done and it may require some outside help to change chronic patterns.

8

Sulking and Injustice

I have never come across anyone who uses drama - and not everyone does – and who does not nurse a sense of injustice, a feeling of being unfairly treated and victimised. Closely coupled with this sense is a set of behaviours we all used in childhood. That set of behaviours is commonly referred to as sulking. A sulk is usually set in motion when we are denied something we feel we are naturally entitled to. There is always a sense of entitlement in drama.

It's difficult for most adults to accept that they sulk. It is regarded as a "childish" behaviour and therefore shameful. It's also seen as being laughable, almost a joke. However, we are sadly mistaken in seeing sulking in this way. At its worst it is a clinical condition and can be very dangerous to the sufferer and people around her. In a sulk a person may self-harm or harm others. In my experience it is more painful than depression which is usually only a threat to the depressed person - suicide is more likely than homicide or violent acting-out on others. The destructive potential of a clinical sulk can be seen in the regular reports of men, usually, who shoot up schools and ex-places of employment after they have experienced a slight, rejection, dismissal etc. The sense of injustice and the righteous anger and rage dictates that "they" have to pay, and from within that encapsulated position any action can be rationalised and justified up to and including murder and suicide. Experientially a person in a sulk will be aware of deep feelings of hurt, a sense of injustice and the accompanying righteous anger or rage. There is usually no feeling of guilt associated with the desire to hurt the person who is seen as having inflicted the hurt and the injustice. In depression, on the other hand, guilt is predominant, as are feelings of misery and worthlessness.

Almost without exception, the people with whom I have worked have one of two common problems: the conviction that they were never given enough of the breast, or whatever the breast stands in for (for instance, maternal love), and they were all afraid of their father or mother however much they might also have loved them. Many have both of these. Those of you who are taken with analytic ways of thinking will see the connection immediately. Here we have the most common problem we deal with in our male patients – ambivalence and the positive Oedipus complex. This is the combination of the desire for the mother and the fear of retaliating attack by the father. There are two other convictions held by people with insecure attachment disorders: one is that their parents made too many demands; the other that they were never loved enough. I will return to these.

One of the most significant aspects of the Oedipus complex is that it signals the child's entry into the social world and begins the complex process of shaping gender, sexuality, and desires. From a preoccupation with the two-body relationship the child is confronted by the social reality that the mother has an intimate relationship with the father.

The two-body suddenly becomes three-body – the most unstable of all social geometries. There are, however, early precursors of this threesome, located more in fantasies but still presaging later struggles with the passions of the Oedipal triangle. The most obvious of these early versions is the threesome represented by the child and the division of the breast into the good breast and the bad breast – surely the origin of all splitting. I imagine that it is already clear that I do not subscribe to the Kleinian notion of innate envy being the origin of this primitive split. Although I have always been attracted to attachment theory I have till now reserved my position somewhat with regard to the origins of destructiveness. I am now firmly convinced that the origins lie in the real inadequacies of the primary carer in the "fit" with the child and its temperament, not in nature or innate fantasy; more, I hold that the ferocity of the bad breast – and later fantasies about other people's hostility to oneself – is a direct correlate of the intensity of the frustrating or traumatising experiences the child has.

While there is much that I am not fond of in Kleinian thinking, I find myself in total agreement with its description of the process of rapprochement. Although it is not a developmental theory, and would not claim to be, Klein's description of the move from the paranoid/schizoid to the depressive position is a major developmental move. The paranoid/schizoid position describes the internal world as being in a state in which objects (not necessarily people as anyone who remembers John Cleese, in *Fawlty Towers*, beating up his car with a tree branch will appreciate) are split into parts and separated from each other. In essence the bad object dominates and is perceived to be hostile, persecuting and dangerous and has to be split off from the good object in order for the infant to survive.

The depressive position describes the internal world as being in a state in which the object (mother) is not split into parts but is seen to be whole. The good and bad parts are no longer split apart with the good object being idealised and the bad object denied. Objects are seen to be one, and anxiety is depressive and focused on the fear of loss of the object through its destruction by the subject. This position is the beginning of guilt and concern and the object is preserved through the spreading or inhibition of aggressiveness. This allows for the stable introjection of a secure object, one which is not threatened by the subject's aggression. You may see how important this is in the context of the process of psychotherapy or analysis as the patient discovers, repeatedly, that the therapist is not destroyed by his/her destructiveness and can be "taken in" over time as a secure object for the patient, one which can be used and will provide resilience for dealing with life's difficulties after the analytic process is terminated. Once developed, the pathways from the paranoid to the depressive position are there for use throughout life as we struggle with the primitive impulses and derivative anxieties left over from our inadequately parented early years.

The split necessitates some process of rapprochement with the carer to enable the child to continue to relate to and receive the nourishment required for further growth and development. Without this rapprochement life may turn out very bleak indeed. My clinical experience, and my experience generally, is that very few people reach anything approaching complete rapprochement. It would seem that we are all left with some unresolved sense of injustice and its correlate, paranoid thinking. This sense of injustice is, I believe, largely responsible for the developmental failure which I have come to think of as the masculinity which enables men to treat badly the women to whom they are attached and, in some cases, other women too.

My experience with female patients shows that these same processes are much more common in women than is generally realised. In my earlier publications I have made it clear that I believe all men grow up with this sense of injustice, that it is structured into the maturational process and the development of masculinity. It is equally obvious that women suffer from the same disability but that its vicissitudes are somewhat different, given the culturation of women as the "non-aggressive" gender. I believe this is why women more often present with "depression" rather than "aggression" or other forms of social acting-out. Of course it varies in intensity from the mild to the very severe, according to the actual environment in which the child is raised and the extent of the real abuse, neglect or deprivation. I do not believe it is innate, although I do regard it, to some extent, as inevitable. What then does a sense of injustice consist of?

The sense of injustice, splitting and sulking

Sulking is based on a sense of injustice, the belief that one is being, or has been, unfairly treated. That same sense of injustice, when combined with learned masculinity, is responsible for most of the interpersonal violence we see in the world and certainly underpins the violence inflicted on women by men as well as the emotional pain inflicted by women on men.

Subjectively, the sense of injustice derives from the experience of never having been loved enough, at best, to that of having been actively abused and traumatized, at worst. Often the feeling is not so differentiated but is the experience of having been dealt a bad hand or that life has treated, and is continuing to treat, one unfairly. Along with the sense of injustice come feelings of frustration, sadness, fear, and rage connected to the perceived source of the injustice. Hubris is often the result with all the attendant self-righteousness and self/other-destructive behaviour which this can entail. The unfairness (injustice) which begins its life in the two-body relationship with the primary carer, is not, in my opinion, symbolised or articulated as such until the Oedipus complex reaches its apogee. From this point on, the child is able to articulate questions that have been thought but unknown and, on the basis of its newfound knowledge, is able to write its own history. There is nothing unusual in this; the present has no history – history belongs to the future. The deep sense of frustration which I believe is part of the heritage of all little boys (see *Why Men Hate Women*) is finally open to symbolisation and interpretation and the sense of injustice can begin to take root. As the child develops, he or she will see many roots of the injustice. From a psychodynamic viewpoint these will all, with the exception of real and substantiated abuse, be seen as a version of the castration complex (including in women), whether it is loss of the breast (weaning), birth of a sibling, separation and individuation, anal struggles for control and self-mastery, or awareness of the father and mother's relationship.

Of course, these days it is difficult to differentiate between real and "unreal" abuse. As a result of changing fashions in child-rearing and successive moral panics about child sexual abuse since the early 1980s, we are, now, all victims. This change in fashion and the gradual awareness of the real scale of child abuse speaks to the problem of whether it is possible to take an attachment theory approach to psychodynamic psychotherapy. It is ironic that the problem which so troubled Freud at the end of the nineteenth century should so preoccupy us at the end of the twentieth and the early twenty-first;[2] not, however, that the presence or absence of "real" abuse makes a great deal of difference when dealing with sulking. Psychodynamically, the task is the same in each case. It may be difficult for those steeped in orthodoxy but it is very important, when working with the sense of injustice, to acknowledge that a real injustice did occur but, equally naturally it seems to me, one has also to do this where there is no evidence of real abuse. In such cases the injustice is an existential one or a social one derived from, for example, fashions in child-rearing or the construction of the patient's masculinity or femininity derived from the models available in the family of origin or local culture. There is always a subjective truth in the sense of injustice. Unless this is acknowledged there is little hope for change in the patient.[3] The therapist simply becomes another one of "them" and potentiates the injustice by refusing to acknowledge that there is one in the first place. As we shall see, the task is to help its owner see that the sense of injustice is a facet of his character requiring constant dramatisation (see Chapter "The Function of Drama").

A great many of the men I work with have been abusive (and this does not mean violent) to a woman during their lives. Many come to me because they are actively abusive, and those who aren't have almost always been unwittingly abusive (not violent) at some time in the past. It was the repeated discovery of this controlling, dominating and abusive behaviour in men who presented with other problems, which eventually led to my establishing The Men's Centre, offering dedicated treatment for abusers, in 1984. As you may know, I came to the conclusion that being controlling and abusive is almost a default position for men in intimate relations with women and that this led me to a paradigm for understanding and helping men which differed from the analytic orthodoxy and from what I regarded as post-modernist confusion and uncertainty.

In the course of many years spent working with abusive men and applying what I was learning from them to my work with non-abusers and to women, I came to the conclusion that sulking can be so intense that it is a clinical condition, most likely already subsumed under one or more diagnoses of personality disorder, but actually deserving of differentiation (see my *Men Who Batter Women*). In many, it is a sub-clinical or pre-morbid condition only too easily evoked with some intensity under appropriate circumstances.

Sulking is both a description of a state of mind and a set of behaviours. The aim of a sulk is to invite the perceived source of the injustice (always another person and usually, though not invariably, the primary attachment figure) to approach and make good the injustice, to make reparation for the damage they have caused. However, if they respond to this invitation the sulk will reject them. Sulking is an invitation to approach solely for the purpose of rejecting the approach. This process can be repeated until the sulk feels that the injustice has been righted, i.e. that the suffering is equalised, or until the victim of it has had enough and stops making approaches.

When I wrote about sulking in *Men Who Batter Women*, I indicated that I believed sulking should be recognised as a clinical condition. In a subsequent radio debate with a well-known psychiatrist from the Maudsley Hospital, he said that not once in his career as a consultant had one of his juniors told him that someone had just been admitted with a very serious sulk. I chose to ignore the rather obvious attempt to put me down and humiliate me (incidentally, one of the main reasons why people, especially men, are violent to each other) and made the obvious point that the main reason for this is that sulks more often than not end up in prison, not hospital. They are more disturbing than disturbed. On the rare occasions that they end up in hospital the presenting symptoms would be of high anxiety/guilt and depression with mild paranoid features.

In *Men Who Batter Women* I located sulking midway between the paranoid and depressive positions which I described earlier. The paranoid position is seen by Kleinian analysts as a product of the child's fantasy life. It derives from innate envy and destructiveness being projected into the object and then a feeling of persecution by that now destructive object. The experience is internal and has nothing to do with external reality. As I made clear, my own position is diametrically opposite to this. I believe that the destructiveness of the object is real and not simply the product of the infant's own projected destructiveness although, to a child, the fantasy of the carer's destructiveness is a product of suffering, which the child has no way to metabolise, more than the carer's actual destructiveness. For a brilliant account of how Freud misunderstood this in his famous analysis of the Schreber case, see Morty Schatzman.[4] Any rage or anger the child feels, which may well be projected into the split-off bad object thereby making it even more frightening, may be a healthy and appropriate (I will not say innate) response to the failure of the object/primary carer to respond appropriately to the infant. This lack of appropriateness in the carer's response can be experienced by the child as an attack, insofar as any pain is experienced by the child as an attack on the self – including bodily pain. However, this should not obscure the obvious – that becoming an adult is for most of us a painful process as we confront and surmount – or not – the developmental crisis which this necessitates.

The infant, naturally enough, wishes to attack the persecuting object (let us call her, for the sake of simplicity, the mother) and this is clearly a desperate dilemma for the child given that the breast or mother which causes the pain is also the breast or mother who is the source of nourishment and love and protection. This is the origin of the splitting of the mother (and the world/environment) into good and bad, loved and hated.

The paranoid/schizoid position names the infant's manner of dealing with the relationship with the bad object. The object is experienced as containing homicidal impulses towards the child and the defences employed against it are primitive in the extreme. Of course it may be true that the object wishes to destroy the child. Which parent has not, at some time, experienced intense rage towards their children? In the Kleinian paradigm the origin of this is in the child himself, and becomes a product of the parent through the child's projections and projective identifications. I believe this is mythical, not real, and that the internal bad object is both a reflection of the real badness of the primary carer (the first external object) and the child's aggressiveness. Apart from that, I find the Kleinian description of the paranoid and depressive positions entirely plausible as an account of how it is that we all come to terms with the limiting and frustrating qualities of the external world and finally relinquish our unhealthy narcissism and reach rapprochement. I believe the route to this is sulking. A sulk is a position in which the infant is overwhelmed with a sense of unfairness or injustice about being hurt, and the hurt itself. Additionally, he is filled with strong destructive impulses and a wish to retaliate and inflict as much pain as he feels has been inflicted on him. He cannot yield to the impulse to retaliate as he is sufficiently afraid of the damage he might cause and the fear of losing the object; nor can he articulate the pain he is feeling for fear of being subjected to more. In effect, he holds both the paranoid and the depressive positions in his mind at one and the same time and is aware that the object is both needed (but not necessarily loved) and bad and hated.

Donald Meltzer called this needed but not loved object, "the toilet breast" – an accurate and pithy name! The sulk is an elegant solution in that it enables its subject the expression of both his hurt and his vengefulness whilst providing the opportunity to equalise the injustice by repeatedly rejecting the object's attempts to repair the damage. I believe this is the route to rapprochement. In a positive process the sulk will experience fear of causing too much damage to repair, then guilt about damage already caused, and ultimately concern and ruth for the object. Lest it is not clear, these primitive and destructive patterns are experienced in everyday adult relationships when they get into difficulty. As one patient put it, "why do I always think I have to leave him when he pisses me off? The thought comes immediately and is very difficult to deal with. It's like there is no barrier between loving him and hating him, and I always have to punish him like I'm in a tantrum and the smallest, most trivial thing can set me off".

What then is rapprochement? I have already said that I believe it is crucial to reach a rapprochement with the bad object if one is to be able to reach emotional health and maturity. My clinical experience conforms to what Klein led us to expect. When there is sufficient regression in the transference that it becomes negative and the therapist or analyst becomes the problem, not the solution, the treatment process is in prime position. In my view this is what therapists should be aiming for in every long-term treatment: to enable the patient to regress to the paranoid/schizoid position in order that we can support the move to guilt, concern, remorse, and reparation. In very favourable cases we may even receive gratitude. I know that David Malan's research did not support the idea that interpretation of the negative transference, the hatred of the therapist by the patient, was essential for a good outcome in the analytic therapies.[5] In fact his research indicated it may be associated with not good enough outcomes and be a negative experience for the patient. I can only say that when I have been fortunate enough to help someone to this point the outcome has always been positive. However, it needs to be said that I have not managed this with all my patients. Also, it has always emerged in relation to effective work with breaks in treatment, and the slow and patient dismantling of the resistances to the strong anxiety and passions that these arouse. At the outset these are inevitably denied. In my youth I would attempt to achieve this with plunging interpretations and they invariably failed and for obvious reasons. The old adage "interpret the resistance/defence before the impulse" still holds good. To it I would only add, ensure that the resistance/defence is worked through before going to the impulse. This can usually be achieved simply by naming the defence and coupling it with the underlying separation anxiety before going on to mention "unacceptable feelings or thoughts" or some other undifferentiated or non-specific and unthreatening state. For those not in treatment it is useful to look for the hurt when feeling angry and to recognise the underlying disappointment which signals a failure to adapt one's expectations to reality in whatever circumstances triggered the upheaval.

The usual process around treatment breaks is that the patient becomes anxious and depressed and will commonly act angrily with other people in his life in a way which seems inappropriate or excessive. Separation anxiety is universal and is probably the most painful of all anxieties in that it can feel like there is a threat to life itself. Often the patient will say something to the effect that if I know how much they are suffering then it must mean I do not care, at best, or am sadistic, at worst. They reason, much as a child will reason, that if I know how much they suffer when they are left, I could not leave them unless I wanted them to suffer. This is the paranoid position and if it is not handled well the therapist can find himself with some free hours after a break as they act out their destructive fantasies by withdrawing from treatment. The desire to let you know how painful it is to be rejected and abandoned can be very powerful.

Rapprochement is the process by which the child learns to accept the reality of the object mother/environment as being less than perfect but, crucially, as being "good enough". This entails developing a capacity for metabolising disappointment – the experience of the mother/environment not coming up to one's expectations – perhaps the most painful of all emotions. This is the beginning of the development of psychic muscle and the capacity for affect regulation.

Of course, this process cannot begin unless the sulk is dissolved sufficiently for the man to begin to acknowledge that he has an attachment to the therapist. This can prove to be extraordinarily difficult to achieve as it runs counter to some fundamental qualities of the big M (phallic masculinity). You will not be surprised to learn that men revert to the security of the big M during times of perceived threat that replicate the original traumas of separation and individuation. I remember David Malan telling me jokingly that the staff at Harrods got hell from customers during the six weeks of the analytic summer break. This was shortly after the long summer break in my analysis during which I had provoked a few incidents with people who I believed were "failing in their duty of care" towards me. These incidents were quite unnecessary and my behaviour was quite out of character. They had involved my behaving in what I would now describe as a hyper-masculine way. The analysis was only possible after I had angrily sulked at him for longer than I care to disclose! The paradox of sulking is that whilst it may be obvious to the outside observer that the sulk is on and that it is a very childlike set of behaviours, the sulk himself can have the experience of behaving in a "strong" way in that he is denying that the attachment has any significance and can be scornful or contemptuous of any attempt to suggest otherwise. I remember a patient laughing and telling me "to get over myself" after one such attempt.

As I have already said, dissolving the sulk, and in men the hyper-masculinity, is not really possible unless the sense of injustice is addressed and validated. It is not impossible to agree that an injustice has occurred when the world is seen through the eyes of an adult who has regressed to the age of a toddler. The key is getting through the aggression, whether it is overt or passive. I am not saying the rapprochement is reached only through the analysis of the transference around breaks in treatment but they are a major contributor to the process. Similarly, recognising the underlying pain behind the anger with one's partner offers an opportunity for emotional development and the strengthening of psychic muscle. If we understand attachment as perhaps the most basic instinct, and separation anxiety and anxiety about loss as the most basic anxieties, then it is easy to understand why this is so. However, whilst it is true that not everybody suffers from attachment disorders, or if they do they are comfortable in so doing, it is also true that all perverse/deviant/controlling/people (especially men) are dismissive/detached and regard this as a marker of emotional maturity rather than a counterphobic and defensive position. Having said this, I fear I may have given the impression that sulking is a disorder suffered only by anxious, controlling men. In fact, nothing could be further from the truth. In my practice I also work with women and, over the years, have seen as many as I have seen men. It is a cliché that only women sulk. My experience indicates otherwise, and that men suffer it more deeply and for longer than most women, and all I have said applies as much to them as to women. However, there are differences in the way men express their sulk compared to women. Men are usually much more aggressive in the final phase of a sulk. They tend to express their anger more overtly. Women tend to be more passive-aggressive, withholding affection for longer until they feel the injustice has been equalised, rather than inflicting aggression overtly. The silent victim phase morphs into the silent aggressive phase much more subtly, whereas the male victim sufferer changes into an active persecutor in very obvious ways that involve active persecution including, at times, aggressive, not necessarily violent, behaviour.

I hope that I have managed to sufficiently unpack the connections between sulking and attachment. I fear a complete unpacking would require a separate book. However, these considerations lead me directly on to those situations where affect regulation (reflecting on and moderating one's feelings) is ineffective and splitting and the paranoid/schizoid position combine to produce destructive outcomes.

9

Why do we want to return to the Painful Default Setting? The Problem of Masochism

No doubt we are all familiar with the idea that there are some people - perhaps many - whose sexual proclivities include a desire to be hurt as part of, or indeed the whole of, their sexuality. When I was a young man such activities were secret, hidden and shameful, but with the rise of the internet they seem to have entered popular culture and regularly feature in mainstream media in an approving, and encouraging, way. The success of *Fifty Shades of Grey* is sufficient testament to that. Websites which display BDSM (bondage and sado-masochism) are plentiful. There is not a single sexual or quasi-sexual activity for which the routes to gratification cannot be found on the internet. Bulletin boards exist for the sole purpose of facilitating meetings between those who share the same fetish or perversion - although those words no longer carry the shame they once did.

I have written extensively about sexual sado-masochism (see *Why Men Hate Women*) and do not want to revisit it here. What concerns me is the question I have already raised. If the default settings are painful, and they are, why would anyone want to repeat the drama which they know will take them back into the same painful place? Of course nobody wants, consciously, to feel pain. In fact, if asked, most will say that the drama, their normal behaviour, has the quite the opposite aim, to relieve it. In work with patients this is a point of difficulty. It is almost impossible to persuade someone that they want to feel hurt or distressed (as the reader may already be thinking!) and there are real limits to the language of psychotherapy when it attempts to deconstruct people's motives for repeating the drama. As I have said, I am often asked "are you telling me I want to feel hurt?" and "why would I want to hurt?" I almost feel that the English language is inadequate to describe the motives for masochism.

Let me make it clear that I am not talking about physical masochism but the much more common kind, emotional masochism. Even using this expression can cause some confusion with people not used to therapeutic ways of thinking. However, in spite of linguistic limitations, I intend here to give an explanation of the origins of emotional masochism and to explain why people as adults are compelled to seek out distress.

It is important to distinguish between the routes to masochism, which I call drama and which involve "stuff" - the attempt to change the present object into the absent/desired object - and the emotional masochism itself. We have to genuinely believe that the drama will result in the desired change in the present object, otherwise we would simply give up. That desire to effect the change is sufficient motivation.

It is widely believed that emotional masochism is a feminine quality and that it underpins the almost universal submission of women to male authority. For that reason it has also become conflated with passivity - another supposedly female trait. The antitheses to these, activity and sadism, are generally conflated and seen as masculine traits. These are complex debates and it is not appropriate to go into them here. Any interested reader can refer to *Why Men Hate Women* for more extensive analysis. What is abundantly clear to me is that emotional masochism is ungendered, and I would go further and assert that passivity is also ungendered. I base this belief on forty years of clinical experience of working with both men and women in deep and long therapeutic processes. In general, there is no doubt that masculinity is constructed as aggressive, active, sadistic, and that femininity is constructed as submissive, passive, and masochistic. In practice this means that men generally defend against their "femininity" and women defend against their "masculinity".

What I call emotional masochism was named by Freud as "moral masochism" and he connected it with the need for self-punishment and failure. I am completely in agreement with his formulation. His naming it "moral" as opposed to emotional masochism was based on his conclusion that the need for punishment is based on guilt. I completely agree with him on this and I will attempt to show how it relates to masochism, the default settings and drama.

Although it has little bearing here, it is important to point out that Freud's analysis of guilt linked it with the Oedipus conflict. This is the stage in early development when the child desires to possess the parent of the opposite sex and do away with the same sex parent. I have no doubt that this is a source of guilt for many people although I think the moral masochism has its origins in much earlier experiences. Freud believed that everyone has an unconscious sense of guilt - a problematic idea, but one I need if I am to account for the constant repetition of the drama that takes us back to the painful default settings - the constant repetition of behaviour that causes us familiar pain.

A colleague remarked recently that "we are all victims now". There is no doubt that the mental health industry has to keep developing new products and has gone further and further back into individual development in order to account for what seem to be new clinical symptoms or new ways of understanding familiar ones. One thing is clear. The patient population (everyone?) invariably suffers from ambivalence. This is the experience of being torn between loving and hating the same person or object. Freud also thought this hatred or destructiveness towards loved objects was the source of the unconscious sense of guilt.

Another analyst, Faribairn, made an elegant contribution to the debate about guilt, one which accounts for why "we are all victims now". Growing up with psychological health depends, fundamentally on early experiences of parenting. I think we all know this intuitively. However, perfect parenting is impossible. As parents, we all make mistakes. As children, we all suffer frustration and pain and we all, as psychologists in training, try to account for why we suffered. Is it that our parents are bad? Fairbairn's (1952) answer to this is elegant. The child has the choice between seeing the parents as bad or herself as bad. This is not really a choice. As he put it, if we are given a choice between being good in a world ruled by the devil or being bad in a world ruled by God, we all (well, mostly; a notable exception is the sociopath, or psychopath as they were once called) choose to be bad in a world ruled by God. To make the other choice is to choose the unthinkable. At least in a world ruled by God there is the opportunity for redemption. In a world ruled by the devil there is no such hope, only despair. Fairbairn called this the "moral defence" although I prefer to think of it as the "masochistic move".

Fairbairn,1952, Moral Defence

In *Civilization*, Freud (1930) writes, "in most other cases and forms of neurosis it [the sense of guilt] remains completely unconscious, without on that account producing any less important effects." "Our patients do not believe us," he writes, "when we attribute an 'unconscious sense of guilt' to them. In order to make ourselves at all intelligible to them, we tell them of an unconscious need for punishment, in which the sense of guilt finds expression" (p.135).

The fact that his patients do not believe him when he attributes an unconscious sense of guilt to them does not trouble Freud. He gets around their objection by equating the unconscious sense of guilt with the unconscious need for punishment. The self-damaging or self-tormenting behaviors are observable and although at first patients may be unconscious of the role they themselves are playing in bringing such suffering on themselves, they can often come to recognize their own unconscious agency in their misfortune when it is pointed out to them. Since Freud assumes self-punishing behavior is driven by and a manifestation of guilt, and since conscious guilt is absent, he postulates the existence of unconscious guilt, equating this with the unconscious need for punishment.

Just as the sense of guilt or fear of the superego may not be conscious in the moral masochist, so "it is very conceivable," Freud (1930) writes, "that the sense of guilt produced by civilization is not perceived as such either, and remains to a large extent unconscious, or appears as a sort of *malaise*, a dissatisfaction, for which people seek other motivations" (p.135-6). Here we are introduced to the important concept of the *guilt-substitute*. Just as the unconscious operations of the punitive superego that Freud equated with unconscious guilt may find expression in the patterns of self-punishment seen in manifold forms of masochism, so it may appear in various forms of *malaise*, dissatisfactions, discontents and mysterious neurotic afflictions, many of which appear to have little or nothing to do with issues of guilt, crime and punishment, but which may nevertheless be the work of the unconscious punitive superego.

Here I would include such conditions as Erikson's (1956) "identity diffusion" and the states of fragmentation and depletion of the self that Kohut (1971, 1978) described in the "self disorders" of the so-called "Tragic Man" that he claimed has replaced the "Guilty Man" of the Freudian era, as well as the "postmodern" hystero-paranoid syndromes discussed by Showalter (1997) and the present author (Carveth & Hantman, 2003). Although these postmodern, narcissistic conditions of fragmentation, emptiness, boredom and irritability are nowadays widely conceptualized in terms of defect, deficit, failures of mentalization, etc., resulting from parental or "selfobject" failure, the fact is they are experienced as *tormenting* by those who suffer from them and, like more obvious forms of self-punishment, I believe they function as substitutes for, and defenses against, guilt. In other words, the tragedy of "Tragic Man" has less to do with deficits in psychic structure *per se*, than with the latent ongoing self-annihilation, the manifest traces of which appear as defects in the ego or the structure of the self.

What I find particularly important in this is Freud's statement, "the sense of guilt produced by civilization is not perceived as such either, and remains to a large extent unconscious, or appears as a sort of *malaise*, a dissatisfaction, for which people seek other motivations"

In this quotation I would simply erase "by civilization". In terms of my model, the other motivations are the dramas and their failures to produce the desired outcomes. They provide explanations, motivations, for the malaise, the dissatisfactions that constitute the default settings. The failure of the present object to change into the desired object is sufficient explanation.

My understanding of the origins of guilt pre-dates the Oedipal drama. Although it is clear to me that Oedipal guilt is very real and very frightening to its sufferers, it is equally clear to me that for many people, if not all, guilt has much earlier origins. We all suffer from ambivalence. Ambivalence is a basic conflict between loving and hating. All other conflicts have their origin in primitive ambivalence. The difficulty with ambivalence is that we hate the people we love, beginning with our parents, for failing us (and which of them did/does not?) and then extending into every other aspect of our lives they can colonise. In extremis, this can lead to paralysis of the will and the capacity to make decisions. Are we not all aware of harbouring destructive or aggressive thoughts and feelings towards the most important people in our lives?

It might seem as if I am setting up a contradiction here. I believe people are stuck in the drama between the present and desired, but absent, object and their dearest wish is that the object would change. So everyone else is to blame. Of course this expresses it too bluntly; not everyone blames the world all the time. On the other hand, I am asserting that guilt, self-blame, is a driving force behind the need for drama and the wish to return to the painful default settings. In fact this is a rather elegant solution to the problems of guilt. On the one hand, the guilt stays unconscious because we are suffering and, on the other hand, we can maintain our status as victims because the world, the absent object, is treating us badly by refusing to change. In addition, our psychic balance is maintained. We avoid the necessity to face the feared object. The secondary gains are manifold, none the least of which is that the drama provides a real sense of meaning to our lives and a structure to our "self", our activity, and our plans. Who or what might we be without our dramas? It would make a rather interesting party game to answer the questions about who we are, if we answered by really telling the truth and describing our defaults and our repetitive games. But this thinking does lead to some intriguing questions about what "identity" really is and whether it is any different from our repetitive and habitual patterns of behaving, thinking, and feeling.

I want to keep this book as accessible as possible and a serious treatise on identity is beyond its scope. Nonetheless it seems to me that addressing it is necessary, if only to enable the reader to put the Mad Hypothesis into a wider context, so....

Who Am I?

Which of us, when walking down the street, has not looked at another person and asked ourself what it is like to be him or her? It seems as difficult as asking - what is the meaning of life? Actually, it is rather a simple question to answer. Being them feels pretty much the same as being you. Any differences are almost certainly quantitative, not qualitative. They may have more or less money, a more or less rewarding career, be more or less successful, happier in a relationship, etc., but everybody struggles. Robing Williams said "B103e kind. Remember, the guy you are talking to is also in a battle". Everyone is the same, only different.

I recall a man I was working with who had Asperger syndrome and was an extremely clever IT specialist. We were discussing who he would be if he gave up all the games and dramas he employed. After some time he said he knew that in the most essential way he would still be himself. I asked him what that essential quality was. "My operating system," he replied, "that part of me which monitors what the rest of me is doing and why I'm doing it." What he was

describing is what most of us think of as our "self" or "I".
He acknowledged that his "operating system" was flawed
and that is why he was in treatment. He was doing far too
many things without awareness of his motives and they
were getting him into serious trouble. In those areas of his
life he retained self-consciousness but not self-awareness.

We are social beings. When most people are asked
who they are they will respond with their name. Usually
they will tell you what they do and give other information
which locates them in a social space - their social identity.
However, most of us know that this is not who we actually
think of ourselves as being. That is important information
about me, like my occupational identity, but it does not
constitute what is essential about me unless I am in serious
psychological trouble. Who we think of ourselves as being
is part of the private, internal world and relates to where we
locate ourselves emotionally in our internal representation
of the external world. Most of us privilege the internal world
when thinking of the self or "I" but it makes just as much
sense to think of the self as being a composite of many
different parts. In effect, there is no "true self" but the self
is composed of many parts. It is probably true to say that
a healthy person is one who is richly conflicted.

The Johari Window.

These simple but powerful graphics illustrate this rather
nicely. I present two versions because I think each has
something different to add.

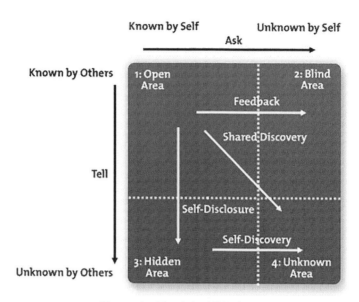

Figure 4a: The Johari Window

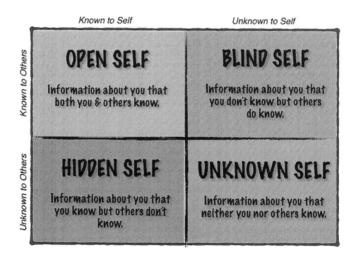

Figure 4b: The Johari Window

The first diagram gives simple advice on how to enlarge the unknown areas, should you want to do so. The squares are the same size for illustration only. In fact it is possible to individualise the Johari Window to represent how much of us is known and unknown. Of course these would be approximations as the unknown is just that.

Identity Management

We all manage our identity and spend a great deal of energy in doing so. Identity management is a kind of gatekeeping as we make decisions about what we think is appropriate to be open about and our level of anxiety about openness. Generally speaking, the more energy we have to expend in managing our social self is an indication of the extent to which we are troubled in our internal world or the extent to which we are in social situations we would rather not be in.

For example, I worked with a young woman who was deeply sad for reasons which took time to emerge. All her life she had to work really hard to not burst into tears when she was talking to people. It was exhausting for her and she coped by restricting her social life and by being quiet in the presence of others. A man I worked with always felt angry. He constantly wanted to shout at people and be generally aggressive. He had managed this without getting into trouble except for a failed marriage, although he knew that people found him difficult to be around as he leaked like a broken tap. His facial expressions and body language let everyone know he was not to be messed with. Most of us do leak unfortunately. Another man suffered from panic disorder and very high levels of anxiety and he was terrified that people would notice. He coped by using alcohol and drugs to enable him to have any social life at all. Although he could function professionally as he was the owner of a company, he was incapable of managing his social identity without mind-altering substances. I could multiply these examples many times over. When identity management becomes impossible it is time to seek professional help.

The fact that we manage our identity is in itself very important. It speaks to our deeply social nature and the imperative to get along with others, even at some cost, rather than face social isolation or ostracism. Fundamentally, the self is a social construction, even the observing self. It is constructed through language. There is little doubt that emotions are innate, although I think they are more akin to generalised states of arousal which also get shaped, differentiated, and named as we grow and develop a capacity for language. Our primary carers tell us what we feel based on their observations of our behaviour. If we cry we are informed that we are sad, etc. I have met many people who were unable to give shape to their emotions because they grew up in families where emotions were never discussed or named. As we know, this is a condition often attributed to men - alexithymia - and it makes empathy impossible.

Managing our identity involves selecting which parts of ourself we can show to others - the open box in the Johari Window. This is then information which is known to me and to others. From a mental health point of view, the larger the open window the healthier we are. From a therapist's point of view, what we urge people to do is to shrink the hidden box so that we know as much as we can about the unconscious. Naturally this is an anxiety-provoking procedure, just as it evokes strong anxiety when others tell us things which we did not know about ourself - when they give us feedback of a critical or negative nature. In terms of my model, the Mad Hypothesis, much of our identity is tied up in the default settings associated with the present object and the time spent in planning or executing dramas in the space between that and the absent/desired object. Almost certainly this is part of the unknown self. Hopefully, after reading the book, those unknown parts will be substantially smaller. We are more than our problems, although it is certainly possible to define ourselves in those terms if we are sufficiently aware to know what those problems are in an "objective" way.

11

Attachment Repetition and the Default Settings

I hope I have made it clear that the "desired/absent object» is not always a person. It can be a job, wealth, looks, etc. What is also clear is that any desired object can ultimately be traced to a desire for a certain kind of relationship with a person or other people. The desire for wealth or a big car or a high status job can all be linked to a need to be seen in a different way by others and/or by the self.

There is one relationship which is of particular importance in the "desired/absent" category and that is a "romantic" one. In order to understand its importance, we need to understand something of what is called "attachment theory".

The central hypothesis of Attachment Theory is that one of the main drivers of human behaviour is the need to be in attachment with other people. It is hard-wired into the newborn child to ensure that the primary carer forms an attachment to it in order to ensure its survival. Certain behaviours are innate and are designed to ensure the attachment of the care-giver. Depending on the care-givers' responses, all children develop an "attachment" style which persists through life unless something significant happens which causes it to change. Attachment behaviour is intended to ensure the presence in one's life of significant others with whom one feels safe and secure and who will be available when needed. As a consequence of the way we are parented we all develop "internal models" of relationships, particularly close ones. These models enable us to make predictions of how relationships will work and what we can expect of others in their treatment of us and what they will expect of us. Fundamentally the model contains our basic positions with respect to whether we think we and others are good or bad, can be trusted, relied upon, etc. We take these models into every relationship and generally speaking those relationships turn out to be more or less what we expect. The way we relate to others, based on these models, is know as our "attachment style" and the one we all want (and yearn for, consciously or not) is known as

Secure Attachment

This is the basic, anxiety-free style. It develops when the infant is responded to appropriately and without parental anxiety interfering. Care-giving is predictable, reliable and consistent. The carer is quick and sensitive in response to the child. The child will feel secure and happy and be able to play and explore the environment. People fortunate enough to develop in this way have good self-esteem and trust that if they are in need of support it will be provided by their attachment figures. Given their own basic security, they are also capable of responding to others' need for support. Secure people do not form anxious attachments; they operate from a position of trust. Most research indicates that approximately sixty per cent of people are secure.

Unfortunately, a great many parents are not consistent, reliable, and predictable on a constant basis. There may be many reasons for this, of course. It does not always speak of a failure on the carer's part. Life is unpredictable, trauma happens, illnesses happen. Any of these can interrupt the care-giver's ability to provide secure parenting. However, many parents have not been adequately parented themselves and may repeat their own care failures with their own children. In these cases, their children will develop an

"Insecure Attachment" Style

People with insecure attachment are generally categorised as belonging to three different types, although one is sub-divided into two:

1) Anxious - preoccupied - ambivalent

2a) Avoidant - dismissive

2b) Avoidant - fearful

3) Chaotic.

Secure (I'm okay, you're okay)	**Preoccupied** (I'm not okay, you're okay)
• Is self-sufficient • Is comfortable with intimacy • Wants interdependent relationships	• Is overly involved and dependent • Wants excessive intimacy • Clings to relationships
Dismissive (I'm okay, you're okay)	**Fearful - Avoidant** (I'm not okay, you're not okay)
• Is counter-dependent • Is uncomfortable with intimacy • Sees relationships as unnecessary and demanding	• Wants approval from others • Is fearful of intimacy • Sees relationships as painful

Figure 5: Insecure attachment style

We can represent people's attachment styles and their beliefs about themselves and others in the following way:

These internal beliefs about self and others are a "working model" insofar as they shape one's expectations and behaviour with other people. Chaotic people have no stable internal models. Obviously, these internal working models of self and others have a profound influence on the sort of relationships we form.

◼ How do these insecure attachments styles develop?

There are distinct differences in the parenting received by differently insecure people.

Those who develop a preoccupied/ambivalent style will have received inconsistent parenting which is good enough when provided but is not reliable. Sometimes it is good but it is not predictably available. The child's needs are not responded to or the responses are inappropriate. As a consequence the child becomes insecure in the absence of the parent and fears being abandoned. Anxiety is high as the child fears his needs will not be met. As a consequence he over-values the other and devalues the self. He needs a lot of reassurance when the care-giver is present. This can lead to clinging behaviour.

Avoidant/dismissive people are generally parented in a non-comforting way. They may be well serviced but the parents' behaviour is lacking in emotion or love. It's a kind of hands-off parenting. There is little interaction with the child. It is sometimes hard to distinguish the avoidant/dismissive from the avoidant/ fearful. However, dismissives tend to avoid relationships and experience them as an interference. Consciously, they do not want to be in any attachment and seek total independence. Fearfuls tend to want to be in attachments but they are profoundly afraid of rejection and invariably find it by being hyper-sensitive to slights of any kind which they will maximise and experience as deeply painful. There seems to be no def-con 1 to 5 and they are permanently set to def-con 1. There is no slight rejection, they are all total rejections.

Chaotic people do not have a dominant style. Their behaviour is unpredictable and this is often associated with diagnosable emotional and psychological problems.

In the context of my assertion that people unconsciously seek out their default settings, the attachment model is central to understanding one of the main motives for doing so in relationships. One's attachment style and the internal models on which it is based contain the most fundamental beliefs abut oneself and others. These beliefs are the basis of the way we make sense of the world, how we understand it and give it meaning. We are all psychologists. We have skills we have been honing since we were born. We are constantly testing hypotheses in our everyday contact with others - this is another way of describing the drama between the present object and the absent/desired object. The problem is that we continue to test the same hypotheses repeatedly and persist in doing so in the hope that this time the outcome will be different even when all the empirical evidence simply supports what we already believe to be true. Rather than change the hypotheses and run different experiments, we continue in our Sisyphean ways, pushing the same boulder up the hill only to see it roll back to the bottom. The consolation is that the experiments provide substantial benefits, none the least of which is the return to the default settings, the boulder at the bottom. Our basic belief systems are confirmed and this includes the validity of our internal working models and, perhaps more importantly, we never have to face the "feared object" and the real unconscious pain associated with it. Unfortunately, this also obviates the possibility of real and satisfying change in the psychic scaffolding within which we construct our lives. Nowhere is this truer than in our relationships with people. Our attachment style limits our freedom of movement in prescribed ways.

Attachment styles fit together. Many of the case histories I have presented are typical examples of this "fit". The most obvious one is what I have called the "pursuer-distancer" relationship. This is a relationship in which a preoccupied/ambivalent person is deeply involved with an avoidant person, whether dismissive or fearful. The dismissive is very afraid of being engulfed or swamped by another and often this is felt when the other attempts to be intimate with them. The request for intimacy evokes the fear of engulfment and the avoider withdraws. This creates intense anxiety in the preoccupied person who responds to the withdrawal by attempting to get closer. The dance begins with increasing distress for both. They are connected by a rigid pole. The underlying beliefs described in the diagram on page ... are confirmed by the interaction and the distress it causes. The avoidant believes nobody can meet their needs except themselves, that relationships are depleting and unnecessary and they would be better off on their own, that they don't really need attachments. The preoccupied is assured, consciously and otherwise, that people are not to be trusted, that nobody can meet their needs and that they will always get hurt. In my experience, the preoccupied person is more likely to become enmeshed in a relationship. This a dependency of such intensity, and not always in awareness, that the loss of the relationship can lead to total collapse. The good parts of the self become totally identified with the other and the loss of the other leads to the experience of losing those parts of the self. This includes self-esteem, creativity, the capacity for pleasure, sociability, etc. I have seen this total collapse many times in my practice, paradoxically with men who thought they were independent and did not need the partner they subsequently lost and drove away.

It is important to point out that although everyone has a dominant attachment style, these are not rigid. We are social beings and we adapt to our social environment. An avoidant can become secure if they meet someone who loves them and is responsive to them and provides reliable care when needed. We adapt to the styles of the people we are with. Nowhere is this truer than when it comes to sexual and romantic attraction, and even a normally secure person can find themselves deeply involved with an avoidant or preoccupied insecure. This can happen for many reasons, none the least of which is that we present aspects of ourselves slowly when we are deeply attracted to another and it may take some time for us to present our dominant way of relating. When two people are doing this it can lead to some surprising outcomes.

Reed and Romantic Attachments

I am going to present an account of a man I worked with for some time. He was referred to me by a friend of his who had been a patient of mine for some years. Reed was very intelligent, and well educated. He was in his thirties and running a successful business. Both his parents were successful in business and had been separated since he was fourteen, when he was sent to a co-ed boarding school - a move which prevented much damage to him. His mother's lifelong depressive episodes, requiring hospitalisation, and his father's infidelities had made his childhood quite chaotic.

At school he had become deeply involved with another pupil in an intense and volatile relationship, emotionally sado-masochistic without doubt. It involved frequent rows, separations, jealousies, intense sexual passion, and emotional chaos. They had drifted apart after graduating from university but to this day they are still in occasional intimate contact and it is not impossible that they may end up together. This is openly, though casually, acknowledged by them.

As he was building his business he went through a series of short-term casual relationships involving lots of alcohol and social drug use. He enjoyed sex but for much of the time he was unable to perform without Viagra, probably due to the drugs and alcohol. He was highly likeable and amusing and clearly formed good attachments with his friends. His social circle was wide and I enjoyed listening to the stories of the interesting people he mixed with. He first came to me because he had been suffering for ten years with an apparently incurable illness which led to his spending days in bed, unable to get up, and feeling too weak to move. The many specialists he had seen had been unable to help and he had concluded it may be psychological. I had seen the condition before and worked with it successfully so was optimistic about the prognosis. Over a period of eighteen months he slowly recovered as we analysed each outbreak and the circumstances that precipitated it. I could write a paper about how we resolved that condition. Suffice it to say that the most relevant issue is that it occurred whenever he had demands made on him. It took little time for him to realise that demands enraged him because he did not have the freedom to refuse. Collapsing was his only method of refusal - his body went on strike. Not long after his «cure", and after a long summer break in treatment, he began expressing very ambivalent feelings about continuing with me. I knew him well enough by this time to understand why this was - apart from the ordinary sources of resistance. I had seen his distress during breaks and his resistance on my returns, and was more than aware of his attachment issues. I made what I thought were appropriate interpretations of his fear of intimacy, his need to retaliate for my abandonment of him, and the parallels with his relationships with women. Not all at once, of course!

He had made it very clear that he never became emotionally involved in his relationships, but that while he was in them he tried to be the best "boyfriend they had ever had». I made the obvious interpretation that getting well from his ten year illness had been part of being "the best patient I had ever had".

Nothing was too much for him. He acceded to every request or want, even to the point of anticipating them before they were expressed. It was hardly surprising that the young women were deeply hurt and shocked when he suddenly cut off from them. Clearly, I was intended to join the long list of discarded objects from his past. I am glad to say that my interventions were successful in that he decided to stay in treatment. I leave it to the reader to decide if I was right to do this.

We had often discussed his attachment style and he had no difficulty in accepting that he was avoidant. It was difficult to be precise about whether he was fearful or dismissive as he seemed to alternate between the two. There were sessions early in his treatment when he had broken down into fits of the most agonising weeping - painful for both of us. They always involved a discussion of his early childhood but he was unable to attach it to any memories. By this time I had sufficient information to be able to make what I felt was a decent reconstruction of his very early experience. His mother had been very depressed and often hospitalised. His father was serially unfaithful to her. It was clear that although he potentiated her depression it was a problem of long standing. It was equally clear that for very long periods Reed had been left with his grandparents and had no contact with his mother although rather more with his father. Putting this together, his need to be the "best boyfriend in the world" was easy to understand. He adored his mother and wanted to save her from suffering but this was a task well beyond the capacities of a child or adolescent - especially since he and his mother were aware of his father's continuing infidelities which he did little to hide and which frequently involved long separations from the family. In addition, Reed had already emotionally withdrawn from his mother, having recognised that she was incapable of meeting his emotional or attachment needs for love, safety, and security. His internal models were, quite frankly, chaotic. This was why the move to boarding school was a positive experience for him. There, he learned to make peer attachments that were healthy and supportive, attachments which he has maintained to this day. His relationship with his school girlfriend was a different story!

After three years into his treatment, his accounts of one long-standing relationship, with a professional female colleague from an associated company, began to assume a different tenor. They were seeing each other socially and becoming quite intimate. After a couple of months he announced that he was in love with her. For some months they had an idyllic relationship. So much so that they decided to live together in his house. At first it all went smoothly but after about two months he began to talk about feeling very anxious when he was going home. It took little work for him to articulate that he was feeling, depressed, swamped, taken over, and engulfed. Very soon he simply stopped desiring her.

No amount of drugs, alcohol or Viagra made any difference. Getting into bed with her made him suicidal with guilt and he was unable to discuss it with her. Of course, she noticed and began encouraging him to talk about it. He finally told me that he no longer loved or desired her. By this time his anxiety was almost unmanageable and he was only functional when he was not with her. At my urging, after countless ineffective interpretations, he told her how he felt. Not unsurprisingly, this was an enormous relief to him and he began to feel desire for her again. Equally unsurprising, after a week or so, the lack of desire, guilt, and depression returned. I agreed to see them together for one session simply to facilitate some frank communication between them. It was a very emotional hour, during which Allie, his partner, said that she understood what Reed was going through and she could live with it because she was confident that he really loved her. I liked her. She was intelligent, insightful, sensitive, and, to this elderly man, beautiful. Again, predictably, after he had expressed his ambivalence towards her, his desire returned and for a week they resumed their "normal" relationship.

Then his anxiety became overwhelming and, for a while, I feared for his stability. He was anxious beyond measure and simply stopped functioning. However, his illness did not return. He insisted he still loved her but simply could not live with the guilt of not desiring her. He wanted her but could not be with her. It became intolerable for him and he finally told her it was over and she had to leave. Of course, there were many tears and regrets but she did leave. So, here, Reed had met and fallen in love with a woman whom he loved but did not desire. Simplistic? Yes, and all too familiar to many of us.

It took about six months for Reed to deal with his grief about the loss, although he was very relieved not to have to deal with the guilt about his lack of desire and the constant sexual rejection of her that this had entailed. He missed her very badly for a while. As he put it, "on paper she is the perfect partner for me!"

Love without desire? What is this about? I hope this will become clear as we follow Reed's narrative.

Roughly a year later, Reed met another woman. She was rich and very beautiful. She appeared regularly in gossip columns as she pursued her latest venture. Their affair followed his familiar pattern of drugs, alcohol, and Viagra but surprisingly, after a very short time, his addictive behaviour changed. He reduced his intake of all these substances and it became clear that the main reason for this was that she was more of a user than him and he objected to this because it felt as if she was distancing herself from him with her addictive behaviour. His sexual desire for her was overwhelming. He wanted to have sex with her every time they met which, after a few weeks, was most evenings. He said that the sex was the best he had ever had although he did concede that it was about as good as with his ex school girlfriend.

He quickly reached a frame of mind in which he disapproved of almost everything she did and he was not slow in articulating his criticisms of her. Of course this was not constant but it became a major feature of their relationship. He often told me how she was completely unsuitable and he could not see any way they could have a future together. However, his sexual desire for her was legion. He wanted her every time they met and more than once. He simply could not get enough of her. She apparently felt the same, as she never objected and enjoyed him equally as much. She did say to him that the fact he always wanted to have sex with her did not mean he loved her. He did in fact tell me he might be in love with her but that there were simply too many things about her that he actively disliked. Over a couple of months, his reproaches increased in frequency and intensity as he attempted to get her to change her behaviour and become more like the woman he wanted her to be. At the root of many of his complaints was his feelings about her wealth. He said she had never had to be responsible and had never grown up.

Hardly surprisingly, they went for lunch one day and she became very angry with him. She told him she was fed up with his constant carping and attempts to make her feel inadequate and guilty. He made little effort to defend himself and finally she told him it was over and walked out of the restaurant.

He made no attempt to contact her and described himself as feeling relieved afterwards. Nonetheless, at his next session he literally threw himself on the couch, curled up with his head in his hands, and began sobbing uncontrollably. This went on for months. He became completely grief-stricken and inconsolable. I have rarely seen such distress even after the death of a loved one. It was clear that he was completely enmeshed with her .

So, here is desire without love, and this after a serious relationship with a woman whom he loved but did not desire. In case it is not obvious, Reed had spent his life since his first girlfriend, with whom his attachment was chaotic, in the avoidant/dismissive position. When he met his wealthy girlfriend, he attempted to maintain it and it led to his being rejected. From there it was clear that he had been totally enmeshed with her and in the preoccupied attachment style. This emerged with full force when she rejected him.

Of course, it was not long before Reed began to face the truth, that he did in fact love her [in fact it was more erotomania] more than was bearable when he was with her.

Only the loss of her enabled him to experience what he had lost. We only truly desire what we do not have.

There is a relevant fact to mention if we are to understand what was happening to Reed at this point. During his treatment he had frequent dreams about his mother which spoke directly to his passionate childhood love for her which he had repressed and eroticised. Importantly it became clear that what he missed about his lost love was her body and her sexuality. He did not miss her as a whole person, but as a part-object or collection of parts, vagina, breast, skin, mouth, etc. There was nothing of her as a functioning mind or personality in his fantasies of her. In fact he said that the only time he felt comfortable with her was when they were having sex. Otherwise he always felt on edge with her. This is exactly the way he described his feelings whenever he saw his mother, now elderly, but still active and successful. He never felt comfortable with her. He was always trying to please her. The origin of "being the best boyfriend she ever had".

Of particular importance was that Reed had no memory of his mother's having been physically affectionate with him. No memories of cuddling or hugging or physical closeness. She was so wrapped up in her internal world and her pre-occupation with her philandering husband that I don't think she had the capacity to hold Reed in her mind. There was some corroborating evidence for this from Reed's siblings who described their relationships with their mother in almost identical terms.

My silent interpretations of Reed's grief and its intensity were gaining clarity. I had the opinion that what he was grieving was the mother he had never had and that somehow he had managed to transfer, onto the, now lost, object the desire he had felt for his mother, but this time it was being gratified. I was not unaware of the Oedipal implications of this, but these seemed unimportant when set alongside the regressive and overwhelming nature of the grief of his much earlier experience of his mother. As an aside, I have always held to the opinion that the Oedipal eroticisation of the mother is a response to the loss of her, contingent on becoming male and masculine. If you cannot be her, as a daughter can, you can fantasise about "having" her. However, you then have to deal with the father who already has her.

After a little while I began to gently introduce my understanding to Reed. It was not surprising that he grasped my suggestions with some enthusiasm and relief. He had been totally bewildered by the scale of his grief for a woman he had professed not to like. Then his dreams began to change. From the previously erotic dreams about his mother he then had a very significant one about being in a room with a sister, surrounded by the ocean. He could see the humps of a pair of whales, very close together, swimming away from him. I am usually cautious about transparency in dreams but this was irresistible.

Was it buttocks or breasts? That is an important question but the significant event was that they were going away, retreating, leaving him alone with his sister. It will not surprise you that he had also had many erotic dreams about her earlier in his treatment. In reality they have a close and healthy relationship. The unconscious is a strange beast! He was not the first man I have worked with who has transferred unrequited love for his mother onto a sister who has also suffered the same frustration and without ever acting it out transgressively. He spontaneously offered his understanding that the whales were breasts. By this time we shared the understanding that his obsessive grief was not about his rich girlfriend [the full, perfect breast] but was related to his experiences of feeling rejected by his mother when he was very tiny, maybe less than one year old. His weeping had the high chesty quality that children have when they cry deeply. This insight deepened his understanding of his grief but had no immediate effect on its intensity. It did provide him with a relieving container however.

There came a point after about six months when Reed was functioning better but still suffering waves of regressive grief and loss, for days on end, which had the same intensity as at the beginning of his being rejected. He had been obsessively avoiding going anywhere that there may be a chance of seeing his ex, but he was invited to a party which he could not avoid for professional and personal reasons. As he feared, she was there. It was like a scene from a movie. She was facing away from him and looking out of the window. Was she really so unaware? He went and talked to her and seemingly they both enjoyed the conversation. He felt very relieved and left the party later without saying goodbye to her. For some time I had wanted to make a suggestion that he contact her and this seemed like an ideal opportunity. He did so and asked her to dinner, which she accepted within an hour. They had a very nice evening without discussing the relationship or its ending.

In his session the following day he said that he felt that something had been changed and that for the first time since the break-up he felt his self-control had returned. I ventured to suggest that he had regained some of the parts of himself that he had lost when she left him. He agreed that this was how he felt. I asked him if he wanted to repeat the date and he said that he very much did and would text her soon. In our next session a couple of days later, he began crying as soon as he got on the couch. He sobbed for the whole session in the same gulping way he had done at the break-up. He left the session with great difficulty. The next session he told me that he had cried for the rest of the day but that the crying had a different quality. Rather than being high in his chest it had felt to have come from very deep in his stomach, and the next day he felt cleansed and clearer than he had ever felt. Also he had contacted his ex and had told her how much he had enjoyed seeing her. He also asked if she would like to do it again. He did not receive a reply for a few days and was very calm about it. He was not agitated or anxious and said that if she did not reply he would feel fine about it. He had discovered that she did not hate him, and accepted his remorse about his treatment of her, and this had entirely changed the way he felt. He was no longer obsessed. I knew that this was very important as a marker of where she (his mother - the feared object) was in his internal world. This was confirmed for me when, in the same session, he told me that he had been thinking a lot about his school girlfriend who had been in touch with him very recently. I have to say at this point that I get very engaged with these narratives. I do not watch TV but suspect that if I did it would be boring compared to the stories I follow in my consulting room every day. My profession is more interesting than regular theatre-going. Also, it matters little how long these narratives take to find a key signature chord resolution. My fascination with human behaviour seems to know no limit. I often wonder if that is quite kosher! There is a saying that all therapists are novelists manqué, but in my case that is not quite true. I began my post academic lecturing career by writing unpublished novels whilst I was developing my career as a therapist.

Reed was not surprised, and not upset by his ex's delayed response to his invitation. His school girlfriend was uppermost in his mind for the next few weeks. When his ex did respond he was upset, but no more than that, and he was able to metabolise it quite quickly. He is now back in contact with his school girlfriend. I would like to provide you with a happy ending but the jury is still out.

It is clear that Reed's attachment style when he began his school relationship, his first, was chaotic and disorganised. He was passionately and erotically in love with her but could not relate from a stable internal working model. This is hardly surprising when we consider the lack of stability in his parents' relationship and in their relationship with him. When he met the woman he loved and did not desire he related from his dominant avoidant style and simply wanted to get away from her the more she loved him and the more she wanted to be close to him. He felt claustrophobic and unbearably anxious whenever they were together after she moved into his house. He did not live with the rich girl/ breast and he felt the same discomfort with her but at a more tolerable level. He felt comfortable with her only when they were making love.

In terms of the three stage Mad Hypothesis, Reed's behaviour was interesting. With the school girlfriend he made strenuous attempts to control her. She was avoidant/ fearful and would not be pinned down and this evoked deep insecurity in him. The frequent rows and volatility were a result of his attempts to control her in order to ease his insecurity and his chronic jealousy. The only effect was the opposite, to take him back to his default setting of profound insecurity and confusion.

From his reaction when the rich girlfriend rejected him we can see that his feared objects were the mother who had rejected him as a child, and the overwhelming grief he had experienced, but not metabolised, when she had rejected him. He had repressed this grief all his life and his dramas with women were an attempt to prevent him experiencing it ever again - with good reason. His default settings were feelings of independence and self-sufficiency, interrupted only when he dated a woman and she began to want more of him. Then he would feel anxious and threatened with engulfment and he would not hesitate to reject anyone who did this. He needed complete control of the emotional distance between them. The irony is that by "being the best boyfriend in the world" he encouraged just that engulfing behaviour. It was not hard to see that he was enacting an unconscious revenge against women and he had no difficulty in acknowledging that. He once said, "I don't think I like women very much". He had attempted to control his ex and change her into a maternal woman, which she clearly resisted. However, his treatment had undone so much of his avoidant style, mainly through his relationship with me after his termination "crisis", that he had no access to this as a defence against his feelings for her and the transference onto her of his very early and repressed memories of the mother whose body/parts and protection he yearned for before she abandoned him in her emotional crises. I found credible his sincere expressions of how differently he felt after he had worked though his grief and I am confident he will be able to find and maintain a secure relationship rather than the avoidant dismissive lifestyle he had previously led.

Before I move on, I want to say something of Freud's ideas about the difficulty men have in experiencing affection and desire at the same time. I will replace affection with attachment as it will make more sense in the terms of this book.

At its simplest, Freud believed that men had difficulty in merging attachment and desire because the first desire and most important attachment was with and for the mother. When a man romantically attaches to a woman, after the first flush of being in love, his desire becomes anxiety-laden because it was first attached to his mother. This imposes a barrier to "lusting" for his wife or to romantic attachment because of the forbidden "Oedipal" nature of his desire. At root, whenever a man makes love to a woman he loves, he is making love with his mother, although this is deeply unconscious. The less unconscious this is, the more anxiety there will be and the more likely he will lose his desire. I leave it to the reader to make up her own mind about this.

12

The Stages on which we Play out our Dramas

Freud made a remark that life is about work and love. It is in those two arenas that our dramas are played out, in relationships and in work. It is there that we meet our greatest challenges and successes. In this I also include play, which is a particular kind of work requiring special qualities. I will address a particular kind of play, competitive, at the end of this book and I will address it in terms of the Mad Hypothesis.

I cannot hope to address the totality of the complex activities that are subsumed by the word "work". It can be discussed as a set of activities, the work itself, and by the social context in which those activities are carried out. It can also be addressed with reference to its internal or psychological significance to the worker, and this is of great interest to me.

Writing this book is work. Sometimes it is pleasurable, at other times not. At times I can feel persecuted by it when it feels like a demand. The sun is shining and I would love to be walking or doing something outside. At other times

I can feel very excited by it, or bored. Those changes of mood reflect how everyone relates to and feels about work.

These changes of mood sometimes reflect my relationship with the work of the book itself. I may be finding it difficult to articulate or express what I want to say and I have to expend extra effort to achieve it. Such moods are not hard to understand. However, often my feelings are an expression of my relationship to the book as an internal object, and it is its status as an internal object that intrigues me.

We all know that without work we become depressed. We depend on work to maintain psychic health. Before I go on to work dramas I need to explain why work has such psychological significance. I can state it quite bluntly. Work is the most important means available to us to make reparation for our unconscious destructiveness. It is the most readily available way of showing that we are more creative than destructive and that our love is stronger than our hatred. Without it we feel unwanted, unloved, and unworthy. In short we feel that we are not good enough; we are bad. This also speaks to the social construction of the self insofar as we feel ashamed not to have work or be working.

Shame is a very private emotion but it is grounded in early experiences of being shamed. Those early experiences are the source of the fantasy (a projection) of how other people see us when we are unemployed. We are unemployable. It is rather like when we are in a single state, without a romantic attachment. Most "single" people feel unlovable and that everyone is aware of this. The shame about believing oneself to be unlovable is the root source of low self-esteem. So it is when we are unemployed. If we are unlovable it means that our destructiveness is stronger than our creativity - our hate is stronger than our love. It is implicit in the above and I want to make it explicit. If we are having chronic problems with work, or even simple mood changes, this speaks to our ambivalence - our deepest conflict between love and hatred. The more serious the problem with work, the more intense the conflict and the more intense the doubt about which is stronger, love or hate, destructiveness or creativity. I can state this in another way: do I love my primary carers more than I hate them? I am a strong advocate of core relationship treatment - that the relationship with the primary carers is the single, most important determinant of the course we take in our life.

Having described, in the most basic way, the source of our emotional relationship with work, I now want to turn to the social context of our work, in particular our relationships with peers and authority figures. This is where the external dramas are played out. It should be clear from earlier chapters that these relationships are dependent for their nature on transference: the projection onto current people of memories, or internal working models, of early life relationships. It sounds banal because Freud's theories are so much a part of the taken-for-granted world that most people think they know what he was saying. This is simply not the case. Making jokes about Freudian theory is a way of distancing ourselves from ideas which, if we were to think about them seriously, would cause intense anxiety. I shall probably be accused of sexism when I say that women and men relate quite differently to work. For the men I have worked with it is an arena in which the most complex and difficult issues with phallic narcissism are played out with both peers and more senior staff. This is clearly not so for women as, in general, they lack phallic narcissism. Its presence usually requires the possession of a penis. More generally, it would seem that people relate to their employers as family members and often start a job hoping, unconsciously, that the new employer will be the family they had always hoped for, and ending up profoundly disappointed.

The most common dramas are those which connect to unresolved sibling rivalries and unresolved problems with the authority of parents, particularly the father, or with the family as a group. The internal working model of the group is profoundly important, and not sufficiently recognised by group consultants. It is in our family of origin that we develop our internal model of what a group is and the myriad ways in which a group functions in terms of acceptance, affection, hierarchy, status, power, authority, control, inclusiveness, membership, sensitivity, etc. Clearly, the more dysfunctional the family, the more so the internal group model and the more so the expectations of the "work family" we join, in terms of those factors, and the more we pursue the default positions, and make dramas with respect to them.

In therapy and analytic groups it is a commonplace that we attempt to re-create our family of origin in the group and will often go to great lengths to insist that it is in fact the same when it is clear to all other members that it is not. No amount of reality testing will influence this for quite a while. Could it be the same in the organisations in which we work? In effect, we can be acting out dramas based on transferences to parents, siblings, and the family as a whole, not to mention from subsidiary players such as teachers or other authority figures or friends. At this point it needs to be said that these dramas work both ways in the hierarchy of organisations. Bosses have their own need to return to defaults!

The range of potential transferences of earlier relationships is no less for a manager than it is for a subordinate, unless that subordinate is at the bottom of the hierarchy. Father, mother, siblings, teachers, friendships: the history of any of these can be a template placed over a present relationship in any organisation, whether a flat or hierarchical structure. Then the drama can start over promotion, pleasing the boss, hating the boss, performance, etc. The key point is that the Mad Hypothesis still functions and the aim of returning to the default position is still in place. Let me illustrate with a case where the patient was determined to apply her internal working model of the group (her family of origin) to any organisation she worked in. Her family, in which she was the eldest child, was a deeply unhappy one. She had never felt wanted or included or loved. She had grown up feeling like an outsider and neither of her parents lived up to her expectations. It mattered little what they did, she felt that they always let her down. They did not listen or respond, and when they did it was always too late and too little. She lived with constant frustration and latent depression. She bullied her younger siblings and was disobedient to her parents. She was critical in the extreme of her siblings' shortcomings - most importantly because they were loved by their parents. They were creepy "assholes"!

Fortunately, she is a very intelligent woman with a rare set of skills and this has enabled her to stay in employment, though not for long in any one organisation. Wherever she worked she was unhappy. Her bosses didn't listen and were impossible to please and she was not shy about informing them of their shortcomings. Her subordinates, whom she treated badly, were rebellious and uncooperative with her. Of course this had nothing to do with her behaviour! I have rarely come across anyone so determined to be unhappy at work. She had very little difficulty in seeing how her behaviour always took her back to her default settings but it was very difficult for her to change. This is not hard to understand. She had lived with these defaults for a long time and was in her forties when she came to me. Her whole world view was under the microscope and changing it meant a huge re-organisation of her internal world. She did relent when she finally fell into depression and her grandiosity gave way. The depression was a consequence of having a sibling when she was only eleven months old, followed by others in quick succession. She had been squeezed out in reality and lost her position as the adored first born. I hope this short history is sufficient for the reader to see how defaults established in early childhood can be dramatised as much in the work setting as they can in private life. In fact, considering that most people spend the majority of their time at work, there is more opportunity there for acting out dramas.

One of the most important benefits of drama is that it externalises an internal conflict. The absent/desired object (in reality an internal one from the past) is projected onto a real person in the subject's life. In this way the internal conflict does not have to be resolved - the drama provides the forlorn hope that the object can be made to change into the desired object. Even if this were to happen it would not change the internal object and the social arrangement would not stabilise the uneasy internal relationship. The loss of the real object would mean the return of the "bad" internal one. I will present one more story to illustrate this.

It concerns a man who built a very successful business by working extremely hard. Significantly he ruled by fear in his business. He was aware of his reputation for being an irascible man for whom people did not live up to his largely unrealistic expectations. He had grown up in poverty and lived with powerful financial insecurity. His childhood had clearly been depressing and it seemed obvious that he had never faced this depression. His mother was an anxious, distant person who was always busy and finding things to do. It was clear that she was depressed by her straitened circumstances and by her marriage to a man who was hardly ever at home and who worked all the hours he could in order to provide for his family. My patient reproduced his father's behaviour and was in a similarly unhappy marriage which was on the verge of dissolution. For him, the absent/desired object was wealth but it was undoubtedly a substitute for something much more important. What he yearned for, the real absent object, was a mother who loved him. He had now transferred this yearning onto a wife who he experienced as unloving and unappreciative of him and his efforts. She was clearly depressed at being in a marriage with a man who was hardly ever at home and was not involved in the care of the children. As ever, the absent/desired object is also the internally feared object whom one cannot change. And that is the most important quality of the feared object - it cannot be changed. In his case it meant grieving the real experience of his childhood, a mother who did not express love for him and which he took to mean the absence of love. Who is to say what the reality was?

The time finally arrived when he had made enough money to feel relatively secure, although he was still plagued by catastrophic fantasies of losing everything. At this point we had worked hard on his relationship with his wife and he had changed a lot of his compulsive behaviour and was spending more time at home. He had managed to repair most of the damage to his marriage and his partner was being very loving towards him. What I had expected, happened. He became depressed. He emotionally regressed back to his childhood experience of being with his mother. To say the least, he was bewildered. He seemed to have everything he had ever wanted and could not understand why he was so depressed and confused. He was finally faced with the "feared" internal object, the unloving mother. From that point the work was routine, although painful for him as he worked through that failed relationship and tracked its influence on his personality and his life. He finally understood that his irascibility was the constant acting out of the unspoken and unknown reproaches to his mother for letting him down. Needless to say, this gave way too, no doubt to the pleasure and surprise of his employees.

I am of the opinion that, although, in the main, people work for money, work is of as much significance, if not more, as a stage on which we can enact our dramas and maintain our psychological stability. There is no doubt that unpacking the ways in which we use the Mad Hypothesis at work can contribute substantially to our non-work lives and vice-versa.

Conclusion

This is probably the hardest conclusion I have ever written to a book. It is probably a reflection of my unresolved grandiosity but this book is a conclusion to my thinking and writing about my clinical career. Hostage to fortune? I hope not. Like all books, I freely disclose that this book, like its predecessors, is about me. Naturally, every book I have written has been composed of my thinking since the previous one and has reflected my own development as a clinician and as a person.

As I have gotten older I think I am more open, and less driven by the need for success, and this has led me to take more responsibility for my emotional life, not simply the things that have "happened" to me. This book is the consequence of that process insofar as I have accepted that what happens in my internal world is as much my responsibility as what "happens" to me in the external world, and that external world events are, more often than not, produced by what I am doing in my internal world. My "successes and failures", the illusion of "triumphs and defeats", my financial security and insecurity, failures in love and friendship. I could go on.

The simple message I have attempted to convey is that we are responsible for everything in our lives, and I have tried to explain not only why but how this message is constructed. There is the "stuff" and that will never go away. We call it life and it continues to happen to us. The world is a stage and we are all players attempting to determine the conclusion of the main plot, and the myriad sub-plots, to our satisfaction.

However, as I hope is clear, our "satisfaction" is not determined by what we think we want, but by what we really want, and that, for most of us, is out of our conscious control and awareness. We spend most of our lives trying to get to the default position in every aspect of our lives. This works the same way with apparently abstract objects. The most common of these are riches and success. It takes little thought to realise that both of these are unattainable and that, even if they are, they are simply one less route by which to reach the default settings. As J.P. Getty once said about money, "you can never have enough". A rich relative once told me that being rich was just like being relatively poor, it was just one less thing to worry about! Success is always relative and there is always going to be someone richer and more successful than you. I have worked with the very rich and the very successful. In comparison to me they were financially richer and more famous and accomplished in their fields. Yet they were still dissatisfied with their achievements and lived with chronic feelings of anxiety about poverty and failure. In such people, poverty and failure are metaphors for spiritual and psychological destitution.

I realise there is something hard-wired in our species that pushes us on to achieve. That "something" is DNA. The richest and most powerful are the most desirable and get to mate with the most attractive and desirable in order to produce offspring who are presumed to have a greater chance of adaptation and therefore survival. So is it all about sex, as Freud is reputed to have said? Are we condemned to live in defaults in order to continually achieve and possess more, to be bigger, stronger, more powerful?

The answer to this has to be yes if we are living an unexamined life. Most of our behaviour will be driven by anxiety and insecurity in a life on which we do not reflect. We are being lived rather than living, and personal identity is no more than a fiction constructed of memories (a notoriously unreliable construction) designed to enable us to negotiate threat and achieve the best possible reproductive opportunities. But it does not have to be like this where our basic needs are provided for. Unless we destroy ourselves as a species, there is every chance that everyone on the planet will soon be energy and food secure.

And there is the nub of the problem. What is an examined life in the terms in which I have defined it here? How do we free ourselves from the prison of our remembered past and construct an examined life?

Linguistically, the answer is simple. It involves being aware of our default settings; the unconscious, taken-for-granted world of beliefs and attitudes and expectations of others. It means giving up the ideas which we hold dear about ourselves and others. More than anything, it means coming to terms with our need for attachment and the ways in which this need was frustrated when we were least able to cope with the consequences of this or to do anything about it except become increasingly distressed and fearful. Our earliest attachments are the origin of our defaults. Ironically, if we are able to do this, we improve our chances of becoming richer and more successful in worldly terms.

However, this will be a by-product of pursuing the fulfilment of our creative potential rather than the object of our activity. This does not mean that "happiness" is a choice. Happiness is a chimera. Sometimes we feel it and more often we don't. Peace of mind, contentment, is something different. I can make a list of what is necessary to achieve this but it may be of little use:

- Recognise the defaults - the chronic feelings of distress you experience.

- Recognise when you feel these - what is the "stuff" you attach them to?

- Analyse what you do to make the "stuff" happen so that you always end up in the defaults.

- Make a decision that whenever you experience the "defaults" you will not base you behaviour on them.

- If you cannot think of a way of behaving which is driven by the "drama", do nothing until you can.

- Never act in your favourite drama when you have been using alcohol or drugs of any kind, including pain killers. This should not include anti-depressant medication.

- Be prepared to face intense anxiety when you do not act out the drama. That anxiety will sooner or later give way to the underlying and frightening feelings associated with the feared object.

- Recognise who the feared object is.

- This will differ depending on whether the drama is "stuff" about men or women.

- Try to connect the defaults to that feared object. This may involve a total reconstruction of your memories of your parents and siblings. However improbable it seems, the defaults belong in your relationship with them.

- Don't be confused by the gender of the person in the drama.

- Transference of feelings from your mother, father, sister or brother to a different gender is normal. The default and the nature of the feelings and your perceptions/constructions of their behaviour will point the way.

The rule to remember is that "we are all responsible for our internal world". This is the hardest lesson of all. The way we think or feel or plan, or perceive other people and their behavior, is entirely an internal construction and a "choice" once we become aware of them. There is no external reality when it comes to relationships. They are composed of projections and introjections. Distortions built upon distortions. Memories built up on fictions and unfulfilled desires.

"Go well and prosper."

Postscript

Much can be said for social savoir faire
But to rejoice when no one else is there
Is even harder than to weep
No-one is watching but you have to leap.

W H Auden, Post-script

Competing to Lose

Why most People Prefer to Fail Even though They Think They Want to Win

This may seem like a self-help book but I hope it is different from what most people think of as inhabiting that genre for reasons that are clear. Most such books never get read beyond the first fifty or so pages - it's a bit like joining a gym: it's governed by good intentions and we all know where they lead! Consequently, I am going to take the unusual step of laying out the whole book in this postscript - to the point that with a little dedication it will be possible for someone to stop reading if they wish and go away and work out the rest for themselves. Obviously though, I believe that finishing the book will repay the effort.

I have chosen to explain my idea with reference to a professional sport, tennis, because it encapsulates everything I think and in a nice neat package of narcissistic individuality without all the usual complications of corporate politics or the politics of intimacy in relationships. Also, this is a little bit of a vanity in that I was a tennis coach in a different life and have retained my passion for, and interest in, the game and its players.

The individual is splendidly isolated on the tennis court. What happens to him or her out there is down to no-one else but the player, and that isolation makes tennis a particularly good laboratory for what I want to convey. However, I believe it will become clear that, with minor adjustments, what I have to say is as relevant in the corporate world, the uniformed services, government, politics, the arts, intimate relationships, entertainment or the high street.

In his famous paper, *Criminals from a Sense of Guilt*, Freud made the astonishing statement that criminals commit crime because they feel guilty - not that they feel guilty because they commit crime. I believe the full implications of this have never been fully elaborated by the non-psychoanalytic community, nor applied to activities outside the analytic consulting room. This paper is an attempt to do just that by looking at its implications for tennis/sport competing and tennis/sport coaching. I believe it is best looked at through the lens of individual sport as the issues are clearer than in a team situation although the ideas apply equally well.

Of course it is obvious that we do things because we feel a certain way. We are all familiar with shouting when we are angry, working hard because there is a reward we want. Equally, we are all familiar with the reverse, with feeling something in relation to an external stimulus such as being sad when we are rejected or hurt, feeling pleasure when we achieve something. As tennis players (or players of any sport), we are all familiar with not performing well because we have had a life setback off the court and can't sideline the distress of it while we're playing. But there are certain forms of behaviour to which we cannot attach any pre-existing expectable feeling, like criminal acts or failure to do something we know ourselves to be capable of. Sometimes we are aware that we have behaved in ways that were certain to sabotage what we consciously believed to be our objectives. It is very much harder for us to accept that undesired outcomes were also caused by behaviour motivated by feelings that sought the undesired result.

During my long career practising psychoanalytic psychotherapy I have grown used to taking on people who are struggling with emotional and behavioural problems which, not surprisingly, often relate to continued failure, whether in relationships, in professional life, or in creativity. It has become a commonplace for me, as for most others in my profession, to see patients, during treatment, blossom in these spheres and to convert failure into success, however chimerical those twin impostors appear to be. Often this can mean lowering unrealistic expectations, which we all have to do at some time in our lives, and, as a consequence, enjoying their achievements from both an internal and external frame of reference. But equally it can mean going as far as we thought ourselves capable of and, in a surprising number of cases, beyond those limits.

I have given a great deal of thought to how this happens and my conclusion is that we are all responsible for everything that happens in our lives. We are the author of the story we are living and we are responsible not only for our own behaviour but the way in which other people behave towards us. Whatever happens to us is what we plan for! We always get what we want. This complex idea is not nearly as mad as it sounds. I normally explain the Mad Hypothesis to my patients by pointing out that they invariably present themselves as victims, usually of other people's maltreatment of them. They believe that other people are responsible not only for their maltreatment of my patient, but also of the patient's responses. So, since they already believe the Mad Hypothesis that a person can be responsible for their own and others' behaviour, all I ask of them is to experiment with turning the hypothesis on its head and seeing themselves as the initiators of their own and other people's behaviour. It's like asking them to provide the missing first picture in the storyboard of their life - what did you do to make all this happen?

And yes, I know shit happens. If a guy mugs you in the street how can you be held responsible? Well, you can't, but some research does indicate that there are certain things that make persecutors select their victims. And there are real tragedies like tsunamis and genetic birth defects for which no-one can be held responsible. In any case, this book is intended to address one aspect of how the Mad Hypothesis might work with tennis players (or anyone who thinks they want to be successful) rather than with victims of crime.

I need to preface this hypothesis about success and failure by cautioning about its limitations. Not everyone is ambitious. We need **not** be concerned about them. Success and failure have both internal and external referents. I remember a colleague who worked with a very senior politician in the USA. This man had become a candidate for high political office but was plagued with recurrent depressive illness linked with the feeling of abject failure. His mother had told him that he would one day become President and he had let her down, a person he adored and admired. From any external referent he was a brilliant success, both in his profession and his political career. This is internal frame dominance. The gap between his ego ideal, the person he wanted to be in order to please his adored mother, and the person he was, was more than he had the psychic muscle to metabolise. Result: depression.

I remember a man I saw who had an Oxbridge double first in classics. He was an underground train driver. He felt no shame or self-doubt about his chosen profession, was very happy with what he did and still deeply interested in the classics. However, he was much more interested in making a success of his marriage and his relationships with his children. Most people would be aghast at "the waste" of his very expensive education and would undoubtedly rate him a failure. He knew this and was not in the least perturbed about it. He had gone to Oxford to develop himself as a person, not to further any aspirations for social success or status.

This postscript is about those tennis players who are deeply ambitious - have a very demanding internal frame of reference - and whose every thought and action is devoted to reaching the very top of the game, but who fail to do so. I believe they are no different from the many hundreds of people I have worked with whose ambitions, although mainly in different fields from sport, are equally obsessive and in whom failure evokes the most painful feelings imaginable.

It is important to understand that ambition at this level is disturbed and that the intensity of competitiveness required to pursue those ambitions is equally disturbed. It has its roots in painful childhood developmental experiences and goes beyond the norm of seeking status, wealth, and recognition.

That is a complex subject and I know that the Mad Hypothesis makes what seems to be a bewildering assertion about success and failure. Much of it is based on my understanding of the workings of the Oedipus complex, a theory of Freud's which states that all children from the age of about three to six compete with their same sex parent for the love of the opposite sex parent. This competition exemplifies passions of the deepest intensity including the desire to kill the same sex parent and possess or be possessed by the other. A failure to work this through in a healthy way can leave profound feelings of competitiveness and ambition. This will be potentiated if there are even earlier failures in infancy such as neglect, rejection, etc. The question is, how can I connect this to tennis and to success and failure in any activity?

Tennis, like all other activities, requires some preparation in order to be successful. I break this down into 3 separate areas:

1. technical knowledge and skill

2. fitness to perform

3. preparedness to perform and if
desired, compete.

- Points 1 and 2 are familiar to any coach
  (or business mentor): know as much as you
  can about shot selection, preparation and
  production, movement, and strategy.

- Be as fit as you can be in the optimum mix of
  flexibility, strength, speed and reaction times.

- Get the diet right and live a healthy life.

Naturally, all these depend on the aspirations of the player. A club player's goals are different from those of a pro. The tennis pro's life is a short one and to achieve means making sacrifices; painful ones for the young as the sacrifices are mostly on the altar of hedonism. There will be time enough for that when they are over thirty!

A professional coach will have a very good idea of the player's real limits in points 1 and 2 and will counsel reality testing in the face of persistent and unrealistic expectation. Where the Mad Hypothesis comes into play is in point 3, preparedness to perform and compete. We all know that, at the top, tennis is about the mind. This is the game between the ears and this is where success and failure get interesting. Remember, the criminal commits crime because he feels guilty. Where the tennis player has taken care of points 1 and 2, losing not being beaten is the equivalent of committing a crime. So, what is the losing player's crime?

It will help to understand the crime if I state some basic assumptions that I have found useful in my work over the last forty years:

- People get involved in dramas in their lives (such as losing), and endlessly repeat them, because this enables them to account for why they always feel the way they do, usually unhappy, in one form or another.

- Behaviour is usually determined more by feelings than by cognitions, attitudes, values, and belief systems.

- Even when outcomes are not as we wished it is not difficult to discover that the conscious wish is a disguise for a deeper wish for the contrary.

- Unconscious feelings, wishes, and thoughts have more influence on our everyday activity than their conscious cousins.

- Most human activity is driven by anxiety. This is not so surprising. Anxiety is hard wired. That is how we survive as a species, by assessing risk as measured by how scared we are and avoiding the scariest options. This requires a high level of default anxiety and a high level of sensitivity to risk. Anxiety is good, providing it does not render us dysfunctional.

So, if we are the authors of our story, our drama, and we always get what we want, however far it seems to be from what we think we want...

- if most of our actions are determined by unconscious feelings, thoughts and wishes...

- if we are competitive and ambitious beyond our limits of tolerance at times...

- if we create drama in our lives in order to provide an explanation for what we generally feel in our lives, the default setting...

- if what we end up feeling is the almost unbearable pain of loss, failure, shame, humiliation, and self-hatred to the point where we can hurt ourselves on court (or in private)...

- if the deepest pain we are capable of experiencing is always and already there inside us but out of awareness...

then what does this have to do with highly talented tennis players (managers, accountants, bankers, doctors, engineers, architects, civil servants, etc.) who have really taken care of points 1 and 2 and yet continue to lose at the highest level?

To answer this I have to introduce a further complication, that of "default mood".

We all have a default mood through which, and with which, we meet the world. You can call it temperament, personality, character or whatever you want. It acts like a filter that excludes certain experiences, like love, or pleasure, or satisfaction, or even want.

This conscious mood is usually the tip of an iceberg of a deeper and more complex set of feelings and memories which have long since been repressed and kept out of consciousness. They only emerge in times of stress or when we are able to create a drama that evokes them and explains why we are usually in the "mood" we are conscious of in our daily lives.

"Losing" is one of the most evocative dramas there is for these deeply repressed feelings and memories of early infantile trauma or pain, whether it be shame, humiliation, injustice, rage, failure, guilt and self-loathing, or simply deep sadness and feelings of loss and paralysing disappointment. These have many sources in childhood as we negotiate the many hurdles to maturity, and most of us have no memory at all of how we became who we are.

Very ambitious tennis players who keep "losing" have these unconscious, repressed feelings in spades, and have spent many years learning how to repress them at the behest of sports psychologists urging them to "take the positives", «get rid of the negative thoughts", etc, and provide them with a menu of obsessive rituals and mantras to achieve this. I believe this is ultimately self-defeating. Fist-pumping is an expression of self-doubt, not confidence or achievement, when it is performed at the discovery that you can tie your own laces. It might make sense if it were done on every point - its absence on the lost point simply reinforces the self-doubt and thwarted ambition. The process of becoming a tennis pro seems to involve even more repression of individuality in the search for taking the positives through the endless repetition of obsessive ritual and mantra.

So, to points 1 and 2 the coach now needs to add a different dimension to point 3 - preparing his charge to perform and compete. He needs to recognise that many really talented, fully 1 and 2 prepared players **"compete in order to lose"** because losing affords the opportunity for the deeply repressed feelings, which underlie the default mood, to become conscious. However, this time there is an explanation for why we feel so bad, sad, miserable, angry, guilty, ashamed, inadequate or angry or a multitude of other feelings - it is because we lost! Metabolising these very painful affects can take days, weeks, or months for the most ambitious (the most disturbed by those unconscious feelings). However, there is another pay-off apart from a ready-to-hand explanation of why I feel bad so much of the time. It is that I now know why I feel bad and, furthermore, I know how to put it right - I just have to become a better player, work harder, etc, etc, etc. Finally, I know how to beat the demons that have plagued me all my life! However, this is a chimera and is self-defeating unless the underlying complex is named and understood and the need to lose in order to account for it is articulated. Unfortunately a tennis player's life is too short to take the five to seven years of intensive psychoanalytic work required to resolve the underlying trauma, fixation or experiences that led to the formation of the complex. Not only that, but a tennis coach is just that, a coach, not a psychoanalyst, however insightful or sensitive he is. It might make a difference however, if he or she had experienced some psychoanalysis or analytic psychotherapy themselves. In addition, this whole project is a waste if the coach is himself a "loser" in the terms in which I mean it here. Some time on the couch might mitigate any tendencies to that and the coach has the time, in a long career, to do just that.

So, what can a coach do to prepare a loser and turn him or her into a winner, where he has recognised that his charge is a "loser" in the terms of this postscript? Not all people who lose are losers, even where they lose repeatedly. The reaction to loss is what points the way. The easy route is to alter the internal frame of reference; to enable the player to see that success and failure are chimerical impostors and to help them to enjoy competing and the process of working it out and implementing it. Accepting our limitations is also an important goal in any sphere of life. Coming to terms with the fact that I will never be good enough because of real physical limitations or psychological ones, and being content with doing the best I can, is a real step to maturity and adulthood. But these are not the players (or ambitious people) I am talking about here. I am interested, as I am sure you are, in how to make a loser into a winner when they already have points 1 and 2 in the bag.

Without a doubt, the default setting of a loser, one who competes to lose, is a feeling of loss and failure. This entails sadness, low self-esteem and often shame and humiliation and self-loathing. I remember hearing Petchey, a man I admire, repeatedly calling himself a "wanker" and a "loser" as he was throwing a match at the Paddington Club. He frequently hit his thigh with his racket in a way which I am sure left bruises. That was at the beginning of a pro career that fell far short of his innate talent.

The coach has to attempt to get the player to articulate these feelings. S/He can usually be accessed without too much difficulty, particularly after another losing match. The player should be encouraged to flood these feelings rather than try to repress them or think of the positives to take away. There are no positives to take away for losing unless it is the opportunity to explore the now conscious, but usually repressed, feelings of loss and being a loser and to try to connect this to early memories of real loss and failure. Just making an intellectual connection may be sufficient to get the player into a mindset in which he sees that he does not have to lose in order to explain to himself why he usually feels so bad. If he can do this and keep it in consciousness he can learn how to bracket it off consciously. Thinking positively and attempting to reinstate the repression will simply make the complex stronger and reinforce the desire to lose. He can learn to separate his feelings of loss from the competition and the game (eg. pursuit of promotion, a contract, a pay rise or a new job in the non tennis world) and see the game for what it is, a chance for him to put points 1, 2, and 3 into practice and to enjoy pitting his game against his opponents without the fear of losing. He can make other opportunities to explore the real connections to his underlying feelings of loss and not have to recreate loss in order to experience them and provide himself with a faux explanation and a faux solution to his early "trauma". Naturally I would not be writing this piece if I did not believe I know the origins of this trauma for most tennis players, or indeed for any highly competitive person, male or female, in any field of employment. A tennis coach cannot go into these areas for some obvious reasons, none the least of which is that he does not have the time to resolve the trauma.

Of course this is easier said than done and is contrary to what coaches think of as their usual role with their charges

- to make them think positively and blank out painful and negative thoughts. Facing and articulating the trauma of loss, even without a complete understanding of its origins and development, can only be positive for an ambitious competitor.

I cannot leave this issue of losing without also addressing why winning is actively avoided. This is in addition to actively seeking to lose. I hope it is clear that all the analysis here can be applied to any field of activity, not only sport. I have demonstrated this to myself on countless occasions with patients struggling with success in their professional lives and in their personal relationships. Apart from the driving unconscious necessity to construct a drama which accounts for the prevailing miserable mood which dominates their lives - by losing - losers also cannot tolerate any pleasure at winning – indeed, will feel hardly any pleasure at achievement, or if they do it will be very short-lived. This inability to feel satisfaction or triumph or excitement with success is because all success is actually a very serious loss in itself.

I can see how this seems a bit mad, but let's unpack it. A loser's life is based on a background feeling of dissatisfaction, anxiety, sadness, and low self-esteem. The overall condition could be described as a low grade mood disorder of a depressive kind but it is fundamentally a struggle with loss. The loss cannot be articulated but is certainly felt, along with many other powerful emotions, when an actual loss can be dramatically arranged. One might say, indeed I do, that a loser's life is dominated by a struggle with the lost or absent object - whatever that is, whether it is operationalised as a relationship, a bigger salary or job, a book, etc. This "given flesh", absent/lost object is regarded as having the power to transform their life; it is a transformational object. Culturally it is the equivalent of "winning the lottery". The absent or lost object becomes an organising priniciple of the loser's life and much effort will be devoted to the pursuit of the transformational object that can fill the gap. But in the event that the loser actually wins, he or she is then presented with an acute situation. One of the main organising principles of meaning in their life is now gone. They now have an absent lost object! This is beginning to sound a bit rumsfeldian and it is in fact very close to the unknown unknown. However, he [Rumsfeld or the loser?] is not the originator of that bewildering abstraction (that honour belongs to Christopher Bolass, a deservedly well- known psychoanalyst).

The experience of an absent lost object (which was previously very present in the feelings of sadness, anxiety, loss, etc) is emptiness. I have heard this many times from losers who have finally allowed themselves to win. Mourning the absent/lost object as it originally occurred in early life, rather than the "absent/ lost object" familiar in the drama of adult losing, is one of the major tasks of psychotherapy. It is not an option for a sportsman or woman with a ten year shelf life, unless they get to grips with it very early in their career.

In conclusion, we all know that talent in any field is binomially distributed. All top 200 participants in any sport or other activity are two or more standard deviations from the mean. Teaching points 1 and 2 to them, or anyone, is mechanical and could be organised by a computer programme designed around the individual.

Aside from experience of what is required logistically and psychologically in order to stay in the top echelons, usually, but not necessarily, from having been there, a top coach is usually someone who got lucky. They took an, as yet unaware, top player and helped him to reach his potential by ending up as no. 3 - or they just took someone who was going to do it anyway, providing no- one got in his or her way, a natural winner. For that group who are "losers", they need a coach with real psychological skills - and some of the best must have these even if they can't articulate them - who can make the diagnosis and set about really coaching to win even when they lose.

Or would you rather teach them to glare and pump a fist?

PS

> As Boris (who never played to lose in his whole life) said, "I lost a tennis match, not a war!" I believe he played because he loved the game, not because he was driven by overweening and pathological ambition and homicidal competitiveness. For him, as for all winners, success was a by-product of his love for the game and his enjoyment of competing. This is not an option for "losers". I will not address here the difficulty many losers have with the unconscious conflation of beating an opponent and killing him. This can generate paralysing guilt and anxiety and a losing mentality. There really is a deep psychological equivalent of the, much beloved to commentators, "killer" instinct.

> Finally, remember the obvious. Sometimes we don't lose; we get beaten by a 1, 2 and 3 better player. That's life.

> As my daughter says; "suck it up, Dad!"
> Be sad when
> all are watching
> leap only when alone.

Citations

On Winnicott's "The Use of An Object"
Excerpts from : Carveth, D. (1994). "Dark Epiphany: The Encounter with Finitude or the Discovery of the Object in The Body." Psychoanalysis and Contemporary...

Watzlawick et al. Change: Principles of Problem Formation and Problem Resolution Hardcover – Norton, 1974...

Eric Berne – Games People Play, 1964, Grove Press

Melanie Klein
Envy and Gratitude and Other Works, 1975, Hogarth Press and IPA

Segal, H, Introduction to the Work of Melanie Klein, 1988, Karnac: London

D.W. Winnicott
Use of an Object, 1969, International Journal of Psycho-Analysis, 50:711-716.

Jukes, Adam E.
Why Men Hate Women, 1994 Free Association Books
Men Who Batter Women, 1999, Routledge
Is There a Cure for Masculinity, 2010, Free Association Books

Jukes, Adam E.
Violence, Helplessness, Vulnerability, and Male Sexuality
Free Associations, Vol 4(29, Pt 1), 1993, 25-43.

Freud, S.
Some Character-Types Met Within Psycho-Analytic Work
Criminals From a Sense of Guilt
Freud, Vol 14, Standard Edition, Complete Works, 1916

Fairbairn, W. R.
Psychoanalytic Studies of the Personality
Tavistock Publications Ltd, pp 312-325

David H Malan
Individual Psychotherapy and the Science of Psychodynamics
1995, Butterworth Heinemann

Laplanche and Pontalis
The Language of Psychoanalysis, 1967 Norton

Hinshelwood, R and Skogstad, W.
Observing Organisations, 2000 Taylor and Francis

Stoller, R. J.
Perversion: The Erotic Form of Hatred, 1975 Marsfield

Roy, A.
The God of Small Things, 1997 Flamingo

Schatzman, M.
Soul Murder, 1973 Allan Lane

Meltzer, D.
Sexual States of Mind, 2008, Harris Meltzer Trust

Bowlby, J
Attachment, Attachment and Loss, Vol 1, 1969, New York, Basic Books